MADE
IN
INDIA

MILIND SOMAN

WITH ROOPA PAI

MADE IN INDIA

A MEMOIR

EBURY
PRESS

An imprint of Penguin Random House

EBURY PRESS

USA | Canada | UK | Ireland | Australia
New Zealand | India | South Africa | China | Singapore

Ebury Press is part of the Penguin Random House group of companies
whose addresses can be found at global.penguinrandomhouse.com

Published by Penguin Random House India Pvt. Ltd
4th Floor, Capital Tower 1, MG Road,
Gurugram 122 002, Haryana, India

First published in Ebury Press by Penguin Random House India 2020

10 9 8 7 6 5 4 3 2

The views and opinions expressed in this book are the authors' own and the
facts are as reported by them which have been verified to the extent possible,
and the publishers are not in any way liable for the same.

ISBN 9780670093571

Typeset in Adobe Garamond Pro by Manipal Technologies Limited, Manipal
Printed at Replika Press Pvt. Ltd, India

www.penguin.co.in

This is a legitimate digitally printed version of the book and therefore might not
have certain extra finishing on the cover.

CONTENTS

INTRODUCTION

DOWN THE RABBIT HOLE

'I do not believe that I am made of the stuff which constitutes heroes.'

—Edgar Rice Burroughs, *A Princess of Mars*

When I was about five, my pet rabbit, Benjamin, wandered out into the snow and froze to death.

~

I realize that this is a somewhat unconventional way to begin a book that is part memoir, part random-reflections-on-life and part unsolicited—and unintended—advice column. But there is a reason for it.

For a few years now, never mind the hat I happen to be wearing at the time—and I wear several: entrepreneur, fitness activist, runner, actor, motivational speaker—I am often asked to share the story of my 'struggle'. How, for instance, did I overcome adversity, in all its different manifestations, to emerge triumphant? What inner reserves of strength and resilience did I reach for when life had me on the mat? Which watershed moment was it, when, traumatized by something vile the universe had lobbed at me, I had, suddenly, unexpectedly, seen the way ahead with crystal-like clarity?

'You are an inspirational figure, Milind,' I am told. 'Hearing about your journey will be hugely motivating for us.'

I'm afraid I look a little blank at such times.

The thing is, and I am not being facetious, life has not been a struggle for me. I have seldom encountered what I would term *adversity*. I have never planned seriously for my future, or pursued a grand dream single-mindedly. There has been no one defining moment or event that changed the course of my life and set me on a path to happiness or success. I guess I simply have been very lucky.

Friends tell me that's hogwash. They tell me that it is my nature, the way I view things that have happened to me, which makes me look at my life in this way. Maybe they're right. Maybe, if I think really hard, I will be able to recall incidents that others would construe as traumatic, but which left no lasting scar on my psyche. That kind of regression, however, would involve a great deal of effort and serve no purpose except to prove someone else's point; such an exercise holds no interest for me.

Be that as it may, given that this is the case, it fairly begs the question I have been asking myself ever since this book project was first proposed: Who would be interested in reading about my life? It has been an interesting life, sure; even an exciting one (at times); but largely hurdle-free and, therefore, hardly what I would consider inspirational. There are so many others—cancer survivors, top sportspeople, first-generation millionaires, breakthrough scientists, acid-attack victims who still manage to smile, and so many more—whose very lives are an inspiration. It is they who should be writing books like this, it is their stories that we can all benefit from reading!

I still have no answer to my question, but since my publishers tell me there will be people who would be interested in a book like this, I agreed to put in the necessary time, effort and focus to write it. If you are reading this, you are probably one of those people. When you have turned the last page, then, maybe you could write in and tell me why you picked up this book in the first place, and what you got out of reading it. I would really appreciate that—I hate loose ends.

Speaking of loose ends—Benjamin. When I was trawling my memory for an early, potentially traumatic incident from my life that might have had an impact on me in later life, his unexpected loss was the only thing that seemed to fit the bill. I suppose, somewhere in my subconscious mind, I realized then, for the first time, that nothing lasts forever.

That must have hurt, but it was hardly traumatic. It's not a concrete memory, but I know I rationalized that potentially devastating wisdom to myself soon after, with the addition of a corollary—nothing lasts, *and that's ok*. I don't know where that came from, but it worked. I'm pretty sure I got over Benjamin in a couple of weeks.

GROUND ZERO—CHHATRAPATI SHIVAJI TERMINUS

6TH STANDARD CHARTERED MUMBAI MARATHON, SUNDAY, 18 JANUARY 2009

D-Day had dawned.

Well, all right, not quite dawned, if you wanted to get technical about it—the hands of the great clock in the tower of Bombay's soaring, sprawling, historic Victorian Italian-Gothic railway station, the Chhatrapati Shivaji Maharaj Terminus, showed 6.40, which meant sunrise was still a way off. The race of my life, however, was due to start in five minutes. Four to five hours hence, assuming all went well, I would be ticking off one of the items on my 'acts of endurance' bucket list; an item that, along with summiting Everest, had graced this list since I was a boy of eight. At the age of forty-three, I was all set to run my very first full marathon.

1

It had taken me thirty-five years since that list was drawn up to get to this point, mostly because I had spent twenty-five of them actively detesting running. There was a reason for it—once I had discovered swimming (which happened a little after I had made that list) and gotten accustomed to the joy and lightness of moving in a zero-gravity environment, gravity had become, not to put too fine a point on it, an absolute drag. In those twenty-five years, I had been national swimming champion and supermodel and TV star and Bollywood actor—none of them, I feel compelled to add, careers I had actively pursued or wished for myself. Through it all, however, I had successfully avoided running. Even as a child, I had found creative ways to skip the mandatory warm-up jogs around the pool.

But life has a way of bringing you right back to ground zero when you are least expecting it. One morning in 2003, as I lounged around in my mom's house, scanning the newspaper, a report caught my attention. Sports-management company Procam International, it said, had just announced that it was creating, on the lines of the New York, London and Boston marathons, India's very first, very own big-city marathon. The property was going to be called, after the title sponsor, the Standard Chartered Mumbai Marathon (SCMM) (today known as the Tata Mumbai Marathon), and the race would be run on the third Sunday of January each year, when Bombay was at its least muggy.

I sat up. In some dusty recess of my brain, a long-forgotten memory stirred and stretched. A marathon! There was something golden and heroic and mythical about the word itself, conjuring up visions of ancient Greece and unbowed heads and bloody battlefields. And I, thirty-seven years old, and at a point in my working life where things were good and steady but not particularly exciting, was ripe for a midlife crisis, a brand-new challenge, or both. My various careers in the glamour industry had each brought me a wealth of new experiences and a generous measure of fame and money and success, enough of it for me to realize that they weren't the really important things. I had been looking for something more 'real', and now I had no more excuses—the marathon was coming to my own city. It would never get easier than this. I decided to sign up and train for it.

Sensibly, I chose the half-marathon as my first challenge. I trusted my body. I knew that with a bit of disciplined training and some tender loving care as far as the right nutrition was concerned, I could get it to do what I asked of it. After all, I had put it through its paces in the swimming pool, day after day, for no less than fourteen years, between the ages of nine and twenty-three, so the basic body conditioning and mental strength required for a feat of endurance was already in place. I would only need to remind my body of it, and its various moving parts, a tad rusty from disuse, would have to be freshly lubricated and shined up. The only question was how that was going to be done.

Things had changed quite remarkably, in every sphere, in both my city and my country since I had been a child, and the world of fitness was no different. Where, in the eighties, even national-level sportsmen—and their coaches!—had had no significant intel on the kind of training, equipment and nutrition that produced champions, in the new millennium, all the talk, even among rank amateurs, revolved only around these things. I had to re-educate myself, and I did. Gyms, I was told, were the new temples of fitness training—all I needed to do was get a good personal trainer, and I'd be set. For the first time in my life, I enrolled in a gym and climbed on to a treadmill.

I trained for a full three months, fitting my workouts into my film-shoot schedules. At that time, I was shooting in Malaysia for a Hindi crime thriller called Jurm, *starring Bobby Deol, Lara Dutta and Gul Panag. The fact that Gul was part of the film turned out to be fortuitous—being a fitness freak herself, she signed up for the half-marathon with me, and the two of us began to train together in the kind of humid conditions that mimicked Bombay's.*

I had expected it to be very tough to get back to a decent level of fitness, but the moment I began training, I fell easily, almost gratefully, into the old remembered rhythms of sporting discipline—getting to bed early, waking up before the sun, drinking plenty of water, eating meals—and guilt-free, hearty ones at that, to replenish energy and rejuvenate aching muscles— on time. I ran on the treadmill until I could do 10 kilometres without a break, realizing in the process how much I hated being in a gym. A couple of weeks after that, I moved my training out into the streets for good. Soon enough, I was doing 15-kilometre runs effortlessly.

I had been told time and again by friends that, counterintuitive as it might seem, a runner in training should not run 21 kilometres regularly if he was planning to run a 21-kilometre race—he should run 15 or 17 kilometres instead, conserving his strength for race day. On the big day, I was told, the adrenaline rush that came with competition and the natural high of running with thousands of others would give the body the extra burst of power it needed to see one over the line comfortably. There were dire warnings as well, about everything that could and would go wrong, apart from all the nasty unexpected surprises that one should brace oneself for. I listened and read and processed and, not knowing any better, did as I was directed.

The day of the inaugural Mumbai Marathon in 2004 dawned bright and clear. I set off at a good pace and completed the 21-kilometre course in 2 hours 5 minutes, with almost ridiculous ease. None of the terrible things I had been warned about had come true. I was stunned. And, expectedly, very self-congratulatory. Despite the fact that I had put my body through no serious physical training for almost fifteen years, despite all the abuse I had heaped upon it in a decade and a half of easy, louche living—alcohol, drugs, cigarettes, endless cups of sugar-saturated chai, late nights, parties—my body had proved it was still my ally; it had still come through for me like a champ. After far too long, I was experiencing the phenomenon known as 'sportsman's high'—the exhilarating feeling of well-being when your mind and body have worked in sync to achieve something physically demanding and therefore fulfilling—and I realized I had missed it dearly. Obsessive by nature, I was instantly hooked to my new fix—on that third Sunday of January in 2004, a runner was born.

I ran the half-marathon at the SCMM every year for the next four years, improving my timing to a very respectable 1 hour 39 minutes at the 2008 edition (I had hoped to complete in ninety minutes, but that was not to be). It was after that race that NDTV got in touch with my film-production company, Face Entertainment, with an idea for a new show. They would love for us to produce a six-part series for them called How To Run A Marathon, *they said, which they proposed to air over the six Sundays leading up to the next SCMM. The brief went something like this: each episode would have lots of insights and tips from fitness gurus to sports-medicine experts to doctors and nutritionists, to help those who proposed to run the SCMM. I would not only be conducting the interviews but also putting all those tips into practice, because—plot twist!—I would be training to run the full marathon myself. The last episode would feature me as a participant in the actual race, and I would be filmed all*

*the way. A 42-kilometre reality show, in other words. Would
I be interested?*

*Would I be interested? Of course I'd be interested! I'd been
meaning to 'graduate' to a full marathon for a while, and
this was the perfect set-up. Face Entertainment had produced
several series for NDTV before this, so the production itself was
never going to be a problem. But the other part? Putting myself
out there, training for and running my first marathon, in the
critical glare of the television cameras? You would have thought
that would have scared me at least a little, but it didn't; instead,
it got me tremendously excited.*

*Five episodes of the series had since been canned and telecast.
And here I was, in the Sunday predawn dark, ready for the sixth
one—that of the race itself—to begin filming.*

*A record 36,000 people were running the SCMM that year,
although only 2000 of them would attempt the full marathon;
the others were running the shorter races, including the half-
marathon, the 6-kilometre-long Dream Run, the Senior Citizens'
Run and the Champions with Disability event. As I warmed
up, I gazed at the beautiful, imposing facade of the Chhatrapati
Shivaji Terminus in front of me, remembering with a sudden
shudder that only seven weeks earlier, this very building had
been the starting point for what was the very antithesis of the
positive energy that surrounded it today—a terrorist attack
aimed squarely at the heart of Bombay that had left over
150 people dead, an event that the world now simply referred*

to as 26/11. Looking at all the colour, excitement, anticipation and noise around me that morning, however, it was as if all that had never happened; as ever, the never-say-die spirit of Bombay and her people had triumphed; the trauma had been written over, forgotten.

The starter's whistle went, and the first line of amateur marathon runners from across the country began to stream out into the streets of my city. I'm not, as a rule, the sentimental type—in fact, I have often been accused by girlfriends of having no emotions at all—but as I watched them go, I felt a surge of something like love for this megalopolis that I had called home for over thirty-five years, this fabled city of dreams that kept a million hopes afloat, this hub of big business that turned the wheels of the country's economy, this grimy, glittering city by the western sea that had welcomed so many into her capacious heart and made them her own.

The runners just ahead of me began to move. I did a quick analysis of my condition—my mind was clear, my body felt strong and healthy, all was well. Allowing for the inevitable blood, sweat and toil that a four- or five-hour run in humid conditions would demand, I reckoned the race wasn't going to be a killer. As before, I had trained assiduously, for four months this time, both on and off camera, completing a couple of 30-kilometre runs in the run-up to today. Seriously, how much more difficult could 42 kilometres be? I was soon to find out.

1

INTO WONDERLAND

'And so he learned to read. From then on his progress was rapid.'

—Edgar Rice Burroughs, *Tarzan of the Apes*

For as long as I can remember, regardless of the social group I happen to be a part of, I have been a misfit.

My first girlfriend was called Anne. Both of us were five years old and in the same class at kindergarten in London, England. She dumped me when another classmate, a black girl whose name I can't remember, told her that if she and I had children, their skins would be mottled black and white all over. Anne was so traumatized by that vision that she had nightmares, and her grandmother had to come to school to find out what (and who!) had been responsible. Anne never spoke to me again.

I suppose that was the first time I realized what it felt like not to belong, to be the outsider, the misfit. But I must have known even then, somewhere in my five-year-old heart, that Anne's reaction, and her grandmother's, said more about them than about me. I'm glad I got past that one when I was still very young, because it was a scenario that would repeat itself over and over again in my life.

Now they even have a fancy word for it—outlier. Unlike *misfit*, which reeks of negativity, *outlier* is aspirational, a word that hints at romance, adventure, a soupçon of madness and the road less taken. I like it.

Scratch that first line. I have never been a misfit, always an outlier. Take that, you haters!

~

I was born on a cold November day in 1965, which I now know was a rather landmark year both for the world and for India. Just two months earlier, on 6 September, after months of provocation from Pakistan in Kashmir, the Indian Army had crossed the international border between the two countries and attempted to capture Lahore, signalling the beginning of full-scale war. It was the largest amassing of troops and tanks along the border since the Partition of

India in 1947, and casualties on both sides would be severe. The UN declared a unilateral ceasefire on 22 September, and the war ended the next day, but the long shadow it cast continues to haunt both countries to this day.

Halfway across the world, another war, in progress for over a decade, took a darker turn that year when American boots hit the ground in Vietnam. That war would go on to sear the collective conscience of America and, four years later, inspire an unprecedented number of its young people to come together in an exceptional rebellion of peace, music and love on a dairy farm in New York state, some 70 kilometres from an unremarkable town called Woodstock.

I will digress for a moment here to mention one of the heroes of the decade-long Vietnam War resistance, simply because he was my personal swag icon and one of the world's greatest sportsmen. Stripped of all his medals and titles (he had been crowned the world heavyweight champion the previous year, at the age of twenty-two, after dethroning Sonny Liston in a major upset) because he refused to be conscripted into the US Army in 1966, the great Muhammad Ali, when asked why he was evading the Vietnam draft, had retorted in trademark plain-speak: 'I ain't got no quarrel with them Vietcong. No Vietcong ever called me nigger.'

Fortunately, not every significant event the year ushered in had to do with war. In fact, it seems to have been a particularly fortuitous year to be born in for anyone who was destined to make it big in the glamour and entertainment industry. The portents were there for all to see—in June, a cult American poet-singer-musician called Bob Dylan recorded a song called 'Like a Rolling Stone', which catapulted him, single-handedly, to rock god status. Half a century later, in 2016, he would be awarded the Nobel Prize in Literature to celebrate a body of work that included this song. On 15 August, a British band called the Beatles performed to record-breaking crowds at the Shea Stadium in New York City, making that concert the highest-grossing ever at the time. The following month, they would release a single called 'Yesterday', which would go on to be voted, at the turn of the century, the No. 1 pop song of all time.

It seems the planets had aligned in favourable patterns over Indian skies as well. Three boys were born that year who would not only go on to capture the Indian filmgoer's imagination like few others before them, but who, to this day, continue to garner unprecedented global fandom through the Indian soft power they peddle so passionately on-screen and embody so naturally off it. They are, of course, in chronological order, Aamir, Shah Rukh (born 2 November, just two days before my own birthday) and Salman Khan.

Even though I have always been a firm believer in individual karma, I am convinced that some of that wondrous pixie dust floating around in the ether in 1965 came to settle on me. In other words, I was born under a lucky star.

~

Of course, I was blissfully unaware of any such cosmic good fortune as I gurgled contentedly in my crib in a Glasgow suburb that November. My parents had moved to the UK a few years before, when my dad, Prabhakar Soman, a pharmacologist by profession, had been accepted at the University of Strathclyde for a PhD programme.

Looking back, I imagine Aai (my mother, Usha Soman) had her hands full at the time—my oldest sister, Netra, was only four, and the sister who came after, Medha, still a toddler, just eighteen months when I was born. Through it all, however, Aai continued to hold down a job, even after a third daughter, my younger sister, Anupama, arrived right on my heels, a mere year and a half later.

To add to everything else, when Aai was still in her twenties, Baba (my dad) had been diagnosed with incurable Type 1 diabetes. The condition could be managed, so it did not make him ill in a visible sort of way, but it made him irritable, tired him easily and changed his outlook on life in a very fundamental way. As a person, he was both brilliant and very emotional, which made things very difficult for him, especially since he had very strong ideas about things.

I might have ended up becoming resentful and bitter if Aai had not led by example, teaching me, without saying the words, the best ways to deal with Baba.

Unlike Baba, who was the idealist, Aai is essentially a pragmatist, a realist. Her attitude to most unsavoury things in her life is not to question or fight them, but to accept. Her credo has always been, in the words of the Borg, the supervillains of the universe in *Star Trek: The Next Generation*, 'Resistance is futile.' In that sense, she is a fatalist, but I have learnt that Aai's brand of fatalism is not necessarily a bad thing. It does not translate to a weak, passive submissiveness to whatever the universe may throw at her; instead, it is a winning combination of three things: a calm acceptance of what is, a conviction that it is not personal and, when necessary, a will to figure out the best way to get around it in a manner that causes the least distress to all concerned.

I learnt Aai's tacit lessons well. I never had a real showdown with Baba—I learnt to stay silent when he was being judgemental (which was often) about my activities, my friends and my life. In any case, he was a difficult man to have any kind of reasonable dialogue with. At the same time, I continued to do what I wanted to and hang out with whoever I wished to be friends with.

Learning how to negotiate this delicate pas de deux with an authority figure, at a young age, has stood me in good stead ever since. Knowing that I would be held wholly responsible for my actions, since they so often contravened paternal diktat, I learnt to choose my actions carefully, take responsibility for them and trust my gut. I learnt not to judge others too harshly, and not care too deeply about anything (because when you do, losing that thing hurts too much and, worse, could lead to conflict). To this day, I continue to avoid confrontation like the plague, and do exactly as I please, no matter what anyone thinks about it. Even Aai.

As you can see, I grew up with parents who had very distinct—and very different—personalities. If you ask my sisters about Aai, they will agree with what I have said but will also add, without any rancour, that she isn't entirely virtuous, that she hasn't been altogether fair to them. They will insist that I, the only boy in her brood of four, have always been the apple of her eye and the recipient of special favours. Ask them what those favours may be, and they will say that I always got permission for every 'out there' thing I ever wanted to do, while they did not.

I beg to disagree, and would like to set the record straight here. I believe that it was I who got those permissions *because it was only I who wanted to do those 'out there' things in the first place!* If my sisters had wanted to do them, I am sure Aai would not have denied them either. And to prove that this is not simply a load of hot air, I will back it up with an example—this is for you, Anupama!

One day, my younger sister brought her then boyfriend, Ashok Menon, home, and casually announced that he would be staying with us. I strongly protested to Aai about it. 'Oh, don't worry,' she said. 'They are going to get married at some point.' I was shocked. 'And what if they don't, Aai?' I asked her. My mother just smiled and sent me on my way. Anupama eventually did end up marrying Ashok. As you will discover for yourselves at different points later in this book, my mother is a very unusual woman.

Baba passed away at the age of sixty-two, succumbing to a massive heart attack, brought on, I have always believed, as much by his temperament as his physical condition. After a brief period of grieving, Aai carried gamely on with her life. Neither I, nor my sisters, would have expected any less from her.

~

But all that was very much in the future. In England, I had just turned seven—we had moved to London a few years before, once Baba had completed his PhD and begun work at the American pharmaceutical company, Smith, Kline & French—and another summer was upon us. My sisters and I spoke only in English to each other, and the Somans were becoming quite the English family, never mind the colour of our skin. On weekends and holidays, my sisters, parents and I went fishing in nearby streams, bringing the littlest fish back for our home aquarium (they usually died in a couple of days, but that didn't keep us from bringing more back each time). Sometimes, we drove through the countryside, tumbling out of the car occasionally to chase butterflies or eat picnic lunches in fields by the roadside. I didn't realize it then, but all that early exposure to the great outdoors, bequeathed to me by parents who loved it deeply themselves, had begun to work its magic on me—Mother Nature and I had begun to forge a strong, deep and lasting bond with each other.

It was around this time that I began watching the iconic series *Star Trek*, which was airing on British television then. The Starship Enterprise and her gallant crew, whose proud mission was 'to boldly go where no man has gone before', fired my imagination and sparked a lifelong love for sci-fi fantasy. *Star Trek* would go on to reappear in several new avatars, and with a whole new cast, in years to come, but to me, Captain Kirk will always have the face of William Shatner, Mr Spock can only look like Leonard Nimoy and none but DeForest Kelley can ever be Dr McCoy. (That was possibly helped along by the fact that Baba gave our television set away around the time I turned eight, and we never owned one again until after I had turned thirty, at which point I bought Aai one so that she could watch me in a TV series I was starring in. But I will save that story for later.)

Another equally significant thing happened around the same time—I discovered that beloved, quintessentially

English children's writer, Enid Blyton. The effect was immediate, and dramatic. It was as if a magic portal, different from *Star Trek* but just as exciting, had suddenly opened, into worlds I hadn't even imagined existed. I remember devouring stacks and stacks of Blytons, after first making sure each was at my reading level. (How? By checking the colour of the dragon—remember that?—on the top-right corner of the cover, of course!) I can't recall now which colour indicated my reading level then, but I do remember enjoying each one of those books thoroughly.

Outside me, nothing had changed. But inside, something was irrevocably altered. I was still a misfit in school, but suddenly, it mattered even less than it ever had. I had found an activity—reading—that I loved, and one that, most importantly, I could enjoy entirely on my own. What could be more delightful to a shy child who, although he was seldom lonely, was often alone?

~

In 1973, the year I turned eight, Baba landed a job working on radioactive isotopes at the Bhabha Atomic Research Centre in Bombay and decided to take it up. We moved, bag and baggage, to Shivaji Park, into a flat that my paternal grandparents had rented since 1942. In those days, people who lived abroad didn't come back to visit family in India as often as they do now, and I had no memory of my country at all. The move must have been a huge culture shock, and therefore traumatic, on account of the simple reason that India was so different from what I had been used to all my life. But I can't recall specifics now.

I do remember absolutely hating my new school, though. Antonio Da Silva High School in Dadar is 168 years old today, but it was already well over a hundred when I was enrolled—large, teeming with kids and, in the tradition of the best missionary schools of the time, unflinchingly authoritarian. My sisters could not attend it—it was an all-boys' school—and that made going there even more intimidating for me than it already was. The other challenge was the neighbourhood itself—old, conservative and middle class, Shivaji Park was a Shiv Sena stronghold with Marathi as the lingua franca. Although Marathi was my mother tongue as well, we had never spoken it much at home, and it was therefore entirely unfamiliar.

With my 'posh' English and my strange foreign ways, I was once again the misfit.

I looked the part too, with hair cropped too close to the skull, ears that stuck out and a pair of ridiculous glasses in round frames, all of which earned me my nickname—Gandhi. Children are particularly hostile to anyone who doesn't look or talk or act like them—conforming is everything in childhood—and I was not spared either. My classmates would jump me around corners and attempt to beat me up for no particular reason, yelling 'Gandhi!' But they gave up soon enough—luckily for me, I was always the stronger one and could overpower them with ease. More importantly, they realized their bullying did not really bother me. If I had cried, complained or tried to avoid them, or beaten *them* up in response, they would have gotten their money's worth, but since I did not do any of those things, they quickly lost interest in me. In any case, I have never been the sort who likes to use my fists; in school, I preferred always to wrestle, to grab my adversary in a hold and immobilize him, when I had to defend myself.

Still, it wasn't the nicest feeling to be picked on by my mates. And once again, it was books that rescued me. Whatever Antonio Da Silva's faults, the school had one particular bookshelf in its library that it had got absolutely right. Standing spine to proud spine, packed closely together, was a series of books I had never previously encountered, books that chronicled the heroic adventures of a feral man who had once suckled at the breast of a gorilla in deepest Africa. I'm speaking, of course, of Tarzan, Lord of the Apes.

Even today, saying that name out loud makes my hair stand on end. During that first agonizing year at my new school, Tarzan, Lord Greystoke, became my hero, and Edgar Rice Burroughs, his brilliant creator, my favourite author of all time. Week after week, I devoured the stories, my imagination taking flight as Tarzan swung from vine to vine, resolving conflicts among the jungle's creatures, dispensing justice both swift and sure, displaying as deep a sympathy for the underdog as disdain—and a complete lack of mercy—for an unethical predator. In this, he was markedly different from my other childhood fictional hero, Superman. I admired the man from Krypton, but I could not shake off the feeling that he was a bit of a sop. Tarzan was anything but.

Of course, the Tarzan fantasy was just the kind of escapist fiction that a boy living in the heart of a crowded, concrete metropolis would love, but the impact the books, and their hero, had on me was exponentially more far-reaching. Tarzan taught me, in a way that Superman and Batman did not— Superman was too 'good', Batman too dark and angsty— what fairness meant, and justice; he taught me, however clichéd and politically incorrect that may sound today, 'how to be a man'.

And what does it mean, that much-bandied-about, much-misunderstood, much-maligned phrase—*to be a man*? To me, and as epitomized by Tarzan, it means living by a set of personal values that you do not compromise on, whatever the provocation. It means having a strong and unshakeable conviction about right and wrong. And alongside all that, it means having the grace to be flexible rather than unyielding in your beliefs. It is a delicate balance, one that Tarzan has always inspired me to strive for in my everyday life.

The other lesson I learnt, from both Tarzan and *Star Trek*, was to be forever curious, open-minded and non-judgemental. The universe, like the jungle, they taught me, is full of weird and wonderful creatures that live within their own unique societies and cultures, each with their own hierarchies, their own strengths and weaknesses, and always, when you scratch the surface, their own lessons to teach us. By closing off our minds and hearts to them simply because they are 'different' is to deny ourselves the great opportunity to discover something new and deeply enriching.

As the years passed, I would go on to obsessively read other sci-fi fantasy—Isaac Asimov's books were particular favourites, as were all works of H.G. Wells, but there was also pure fantasy—books and series like *Game of Thrones*, The Lord of the Rings and Harry Potter. I would also end up reading at least 200 Mills & Boon romances as a young teenager—you must remember that I had three sisters. My mom read a ton of M & B as well—she had been educated in a Marathi-medium school and used the books to improve her English. No, seriously.

I read much less now, if ever, and contemporary fiction simply does not hold my attention. But hand me a Tarzan book any time, and I will set off, swinging through the

African jungle with my hero, keeping my eyes peeled for danger. And when I spot it, I will fill my lungs, throw my head back and let fly the warning cry of the great apes for the creatures of the jungle to hear and heed—*Kreegah bundolo!*

KILOMETRE 19.7—SHIVAJI PARK

6TH STANDARD CHARTERED MUMBAI MARATHON, SUNDAY, 18 JANUARY 2009

Starting off strongly from the UNESCO World Heritage Site of Chhatrapati Shivaji Terminus, I made my way south through the historic Fort area before I hung a right, skirting the northern borders of the Oval Maidan and the Brabourne Stadium to come face-to-face with the broad, steadily lightening sweep of Back Bay. Left on Marine Drive then, all the way to Nariman Point, until, at the Oberoi Hotel—custodian of so many of my memories from long-ago fashion shows and another venue where the horrors of 26/11 had unfolded—the route turned back on itself and the long straight began, going steadily north into the city.

The modern big-city marathon is a whole lot more than a bunch of freaks running a 42-kilometre race. It is about a city coming together in a raucous celebration of itself, a community-wide festival that has people spilling out of their homes and into the streets, all barriers of race, religion and social, economic and political differences forgotten, to cheer thousands of other people for the sheer joy of it. It is also an occasion to create visibility and raise some serious money for deserving causes and charities. I had always run to raise money for multiple sclerosis, and this year was no different. I hoped that my taking on the challenge of the full marathon would create even more awareness about the terrible condition.

Apart from all this, however, the modern marathon is also a great opportunity for the host city to showcase those bits of its geography that tell a particular story about itself to the world—its wide boulevards and skyscrapers, its charming old neighbourhoods and upscale shopping districts, its natural gifts and historical monuments. Ever since 1976, when the founder of the New York Marathon, Fred Lebow, following the suggestion of a civil servant called George Spitz, decided to change the route of the NYC Marathon from the original four-lap circuit of Central Park to a route that took runners through all five boroughs of the city—it was supposed to be a special edition, to commemorate the bicentennial of American independence, but it proved so successful that it stuck—the marathon route has become a huge and much-debated part of every well-known city marathon.

I ran comfortably, at a steady 6 kmph, following the curve of the bay along the Queen's Necklace for 4.5 kilometres, thinking of the thousands of concrete tetrapods—those weird, four-legged guardsmen—that shored up the city's most beautiful promenade against a sea from which so much of it had been reclaimed. When the road began to curve up into upscale Malabar Hill at Girgaum Chowpatty, I was tempted to run up there to watch the sun light up the sea as it rose, but there was more sea to come ahead of me. So, with the rest of the runners, I turned right towards Hughes Road, jogging past the August Kranti Maidan and over independent India's very first flyover, built in 1965, to Kemp's Corner. Up Cumballa Hill next at Peddar Road, past the homes of the very rich and (quite often) famous, and down past Cadbury House, where the first hoarding with my face on it had gone up in 1989. Thence to Haji Ali, past the elegant masjid-in-the-sea and the famous, eponymous juice shop where I had first seen Shah Rukh Khan in the flesh, one long-ago night, dancing on top of a jeep.

An hour later, as I passed the Nehru Planetarium and the iconic 125-year-old Mahalaxmi Race Course and began to close in on the 12-kilometre mark, I was feeling good and going well. My target time to complete the 42.16 kilometres was 3 hours 45 minutes, and so far, I was on course. I had worked up quite a sweat by now, but that in itself didn't bother me; I was, had always been, a big sweat-er. What was beginning to concern me a little was the heat, which, at only 7.45 a.m., was already starting to make its presence felt.

To take my mind off the heat, I began to think about, erm, sweat. People make a big deal of sweat—there is constant talk of how much it smells, how many germs it breeds, how it blocks your pores and gives you blackheads, how it makes you itch and how very uncomfortable it is to be bathed in it. You are constantly assailed by products that promise to make you sweat less or help your sweaty bits smell less gross. Here's the thing, though—sweating is simply an indication that your body's temperature-control system is working well. Also— surprise, surprise!—human sweat is completely odourless. I was a h-u-g-e sweat-er, but I never used deodorant. Actually, I used almost no 'products' on my body or hair—I shampooed my hair once a month, and I hadn't used shaving foam, cologne, sunblock or, hold your breath, soap, in over ten years.

No, seriously.

People are aghast when I tell them this, completely disbelieving—surely, they tell me, you must use something *to clean yourself? Shikakai? Besan mixed with curd? When I reply in the negative, they want to know why. Am I allergic to stuff in soap? They could recommend hypoallergenic soaps! Do perfumed products give me a headache? They knew of soaps and shampoos that smell completely natural! I usually burst out laughing at this point—what could possibly smell more completely natural than my own sweat, my own signature scent? As long as the odour wasn't offensive—and I was pretty sure mine wasn't— why would I want to smell like flowers or lemons or pine trees instead of like, well, myself?*

And then of course comes the inevitable: 'But you were a supermodel!' Yes, and what of it? If a shy teenager who absolutely hated being photographed could become a supermodel, surely a supermodel who once used a ton of products could just as easily turn into a proselytizer for the no-soap life!

In the past five years, since I had first started running seriously, I had become an iconoclast in other ways as well. After a long hiatus from the solitary, disciplined life of a competitive swimmer—a hiatus I had spent exploring the strange and surreal (to me, at least) fantasy worlds of modelling, television and film—I had returned to my comfort zone, which meant that a lot of things had reverted to the default 'the way things were' setting. Despite the commonly held wisdom that networking and being visible was important to actors and models, I had completely dropped out of the social scene. I had given up smoking entirely and did not drink even socially. When I did go to parties hosted by close friends in the movie and glamour industries, I dressed with precious little regard for fashion and plenty for comfort. In the beginning, people were genuinely concerned—they urged me to dress better, wear nice shoes, colour my hair and maybe, just maybe, condition it occasionally? I invariably laughed off their suggestions, leaving them even more concerned than before.

By and by, however, my friends understood what my family had always known—I wasn't dressing down and keeping it simple because I was unhappy or seeking attention; this was simply who I was. They realized that the person they knew had changed not a whit, he had simply stopped pandering to other people's expectations of him. Eventually, they relaxed and accepted me in my new version (which was really my old version, only they didn't know it). It was truly liberating for all concerned, and it taught me a valuable lesson—if you stick smilingly to what you believe in, without getting defensive or worrying about whether people will accept you, they eventually will.

I hit 12 kilometres, and the chatter in my head slowed to a halt as I emerged from Khan Abdul Ghaffar Khan Marg on to Worli Sea Face and the breathtaking panorama of the Arabian Sea, awash in the glittering sunlight. A steady 2 kilometres along the Sea Face; then, at 14 kilometres, past the Worli entrance to the Sea Link, I checked my watch—1 hour 16 minutes. Excellent. A smooth U-turn, and I was running down the waterfront in the opposite direction. With other runners, and the occasional palms, obscuring the sight of the water, my thoughts started up again. I was sweating buckets now, so naturally, my mind went straight back to the question of hygiene.

My understanding of hygiene probably sounds unconventional, even radical, but it has worked well for me. This is how I think about it. (My beliefs are inspired by my own experience and by expert opinion, including those of doctors, like the cardiologist Dr B.M. Hegde. If you haven't heard him debunk myths around modern medicine, you should. I'm a fan.)

- *Human sweat itself is odourless. What makes it smell offensive are the acids that are released when the bacteria that live on our skin get to work on our sweat.*

- *Breaking down sweat into acid takes time and can only happen if the sweat isn't allowed to dry naturally in the open air—i.e., if you are wearing constricting clothes or clothes in a material that doesn't 'breathe'—or if you don't keep your sweaty areas clean.*

- *You can get your sweaty areas clean simply by rinsing and scrubbing yourself with good old water a couple of times a day, or more if you have been sweating more than usual.*

- *The highly marketed 'germ-killing' soaps are not only not beneficial, they are actively harmful, because, well,* they're killing your germs! *We are absolutely covered, both inside and out, with germs—they comprise over 60 per cent of the human body—and if they were so bad for us, evolution would have got rid of them (or us!) long before now. In fact, we have a really healthy, happy and symbiotic relationship with our germs. So use water, by all means, to get rid of dirt and grime, but leave your germs alone.*

- *Our germs release certain smells in certain conditions— any imbalance in our diets, our stress levels or our emotional states can cause them to react in an abnormal way. 'Animals can smell fear' is not just an expression, it's the honest-to-goodness truth. If you're eating the right kinds of foods, doing whatever it takes to keep your mental and emotional states balanced, and rinsing and scrubbing yourself regularly, you really don't need to do any more.*

~

Away from the sea now, and back into the city. But no matter— even when you can't see it, the sea is always present in Bombay, in the sharp smell of bombil drying in the sun, in the salty air that finds its way into the bhelpuri, in the way your clothes cling to your back, wet with sweat, even when you are doing nothing more strenuous than strolling, in the rejuvenating breeze that gaily lifts the same clothes off your back come evening.

I headed further north and into Prabhadevi via Dr Annie Besant Road, pausing only for a quick mental genuflection to Mumbai's most beloved deity as I went past Siddhivinayak Temple: keep a beady eye out for me, will you, Ganapati Bappa? I meant it too—I was feeling a bit of a strain on my right calf muscle and was hoping like heck it wouldn't develop into something worse.

19.7 kilometres, and I'm back in my hood, Shivaji Park. When we returned from England, these were the streets that had welcomed my family and me home. This was where I grew up, and where Aai still lived. To my right was the sprawl of the

Park itself; on my left, out of sight, lay the Mahatma Gandhi Memorial Swimming Pool, where the furious flailing of my eight-year-old self had first attracted the attention of a coach. This, truly, was where it had all begun.

I felt my heart fill with gratitude for parents who had allowed me to stay with sport, with swimming, for longer than anyone else in the family had thought wise. If it hadn't been for those years in the pool, not only would I not be running this race today, so comfortably, but I would also be a completely different, less evolved human being. Of that, I had no doubt.

I checked my watch again. A little under two hours gone, and a kilometre or so to the halfway mark. The strain on my right calf was a bit more evident now, but it wasn't hampering my run.

Yet.

Quickly, I banished the thought. Keep moving!

2

LIKE A FISH TO WATER

'It's just a job. Grass grows, birds fly, waves pound the sand. I beat people up.'

—Muhammad Ali

The most consistent background theme of my teenage years, the thing that ran like a shimmering, unbroken thread through the fabric of my sometimes-turbulent adolescent life—my first serious relationships, my SSC and 12th-grade boards, my unchecked fits of rage—was swimming.

In 1984, at the age of eighteen, I would become the Indian Men's Breaststroke National Champion in the 100-metre breaststroke and would go on to defend my title successfully for the next four years. But if I think back to all the time I spent busting my butt in training—from ages nine to twenty-three—I don't remember that I enjoyed it particularly.

Swimming was never a *passion*—it was just something I did, as regularly, as unquestioningly and as uncomplainingly as going to school or swotting for my exams. Sure, it was something I got very good at eventually, and I certainly enjoyed winning, but since it had never been something I had picked out for myself, it never engaged my heart completely. Maybe that's why it was so easy to walk away from it when I did.

Looking back, though, I realize how much those years of relentless swimming taught me and what a huge role they played in making me the person I am today. That may be part of the reason I believe that planning your future is overrated; sometimes, when you allow life to do its thing, it could take you on adventures you had never dreamt possible.

Swimming is also the reason I mistrust what the French call *la grande passion*, the big consuming love for something that is often quoted by acolytes of the 'follow-your-dream' school as the fundamental reason for success and, more importantly, happiness. In my experience, it is more often the dispassionate pegging away at something, day in and day out, that makes the magic happen.

~

It was purely an accident of circumstance. For some reason, the powers that be in the city of Bombay had decided that my neighbourhood, Shivaji Park, was the perfect place in which to plonk a 50-metre Olympic-sized public swimming pool. My parents, looking for ways to keep a nine-year-old gainfully occupied and out of mischief after school hours, promptly enrolled me as a member. Given that this was the only large public pool in a 10-kilometre radius, there must have been at least 10,000 other members, but that was not something that bothered them.

It bothered me, though. Most times, there was just enough room in the teeming pool to dog-paddle in place, and my inflatable armbands just made it worse. One day, even before I had got my floaters on, a friend shoved me into the deep end. He thought it was funny. I certainly did not, but I managed to get out with my life intact—and luckily, with no newly induced fear of the water.

My flailing and floundering had attracted the attention of the coach, Percy Hakim, though, and he casually suggested that I sign up for the coaching programme. There was a very tempting hook—those in the programme got a strip of pool exclusively to themselves, where it was actually possible to swim a few feet without bumping into someone else. Plus, the children's coaching happened during the ladies' time, when the pool was less crowded. I agreed with alacrity. The rest is history.

In that very first year of training, at the age of ten, I won my first national-level medal, a silver, at the under-11 championships. It was all the incentive a lad needed. Even though I did not win again at the national level until I was fifteen, I kept at it. After all, I was the fastest in my category at the state level, and there was always the next tournament to work towards.

That first medal was very special, though, and not just because of how it felt to win at the highest level so soon after I had first stepped into a proper swimming pool. For the nationals that year, my Maharashtra teammates and I had to travel to Punjab. Because I was still so little, Aai came along. I remember vividly the huge excitement of being bundled into a bus with the entire team, after the championships were done, to visit the engineering marvel that was the Bhakra–Nangal Dam. (Inexplicably, 'sightseeing' was never a part of any other nationals after that.)

The sardar who had organized the trip for us was a jolly chap, who, as it turned out, was also an amateur palm-reader. He offered to look at my palm on the bus and, after he had studied it for a few minutes, turned to Aai and told her it was my destiny to always be surrounded by women. Aai nodded, smiling, and didn't think too much of it. After all, with three sisters, that was my current—and therefore future—reality. She never guessed, and neither did I, just how prescient that sardarji's words would turn out to be. To this day, she cannot understand—and does not hesitate to let me know it!—why any woman in her right mind would find me attractive. Hah!

The other thing that happened around the time I started swimming was my enrolment with the Rashtriya Swayamsevak Sangh, or the RSS. Once again, it was all about location, location, location. The local *shakha*, or training centre, was at Shivaji Park itself, and Baba was a great believer in the benefits that would accrue to a young boy, in terms of disciplined living, physical fitness and right thinking, from being part of the junior cadres of the RSS. Also, it was just something many young boys in the neighbourhood did—a very Shivaji Park thing.

For a long time after I'd been enrolled, I hid out on the sidelines, concealed by a convenient hedge. I was annoyed that my parents had pushed a happy loner like me into forced activities with other children, without so much as a by-your-leave, and I wanted no part of it. My usual companions on the bench were an elderly Anglo-Indian couple and their boxer, Jeeves. One day, Aunty Prudence got so concerned about me hanging around by myself that she insisted on accompanying me home. When Aai came to the door (I think Aunty Prudence was most relieved to find that I hadn't been lying, that I really did have a home and a mother who cared about me), she told her what I had really been doing each evening.

Of course, after that, there was no escape from the shakha. The nice outcome—there's always one, if you only care to look—of this whole episode was that I made two—rather, *three*—wonderful friends. It became my job to walk Jeeves every evening, and so I did, very happily, for the rest of his life.

When I read today all the subversive, communal propaganda the media attributes to RSS shakhas, I am frankly baffled. My memories of what happened at our shakha between 6 and 7 p.m. each weekday evening are completely different—we marched about in our khaki shorts, did some yoga, worked out in a traditional outdoor gymnasium with no fancy equipment, sang songs and chanted Sanskrit verses that we did not understand the meanings of, played games and had a bunch of fun with our fellows. Occasionally, we'd be taken on treks or overnight camping trips in the hills around Bombay, which we eagerly looked forward to and enjoyed very much.

The whole thing was overseen by a team of mostly-well-meaning—if not always inspirational—adults, who truly believed they were helping raise good 'civilian soldiers'—boys respectful of authority, well-behaved in the presence of adults and well-aware of the importance of physical fitness—who would put their efforts into nation-building when they grew up. A desi Scouts movement, if you will.

As for the parents who registered their kids, most saw the shakha as just another way to keep their offspring in good shape and out of trouble. My dad had been part of the RSS himself and was a proud Hindu. I didn't see what there was to be proud about, but on the other hand, I didn't see that there was much to complain about either. It just was. I don't know what my shakha leaders felt about being Hindu—they didn't really air their views on it to us, as far as I remember. Even if they had, I would not have paid attention—it would have made them sound too much like my dad.

~

After the initial—admittedly tough—period of adjustment, school life passed in a comfortable blur. I did not find my lessons difficult. Although I struggled somewhat with maths, I was pretty much at the top of the class when it came to English, physics, biology and the social sciences. I was never any trouble, and my teachers liked me. I was very good at elocution and decent at sport, although I must confess (as I already have before) that I absolutely detested running. Outside school, it was Ajit Wadekar and Sunil Gavaskar who ruled Indian hearts and minds, but inside, it was football that was the more popular sport. In any case, I wasn't interested in either. Strangely enough, I did very much enjoy listening to the cricket commentary on the radio, never mind that I didn't quite understand the rules of the game until I was much older. I think I found out what 'lbw' meant only when I was well into my teens. I still haven't figured out the rules of football.

I suppose team sports have never interested me much. My wife, Ankita, thinks it is because I have trust issues, and maybe she's right. I have always been a pretty solitary kind of guy—happiest in my own company. I have never understood why people find being alone uncomfortable. I crave it, seek it actively. A few years ago, I bought Aai a holiday home in a quiet part of Lonavla, overlooking a beautiful valley. When she travels there, which is seldom, she goes with one or more of my sisters and their families. I go there more often, whenever I am in town and have a couple of days off, and I always go alone.

I don't like to cook at all, so I've made sure there is a caretaker there who is also a very good cook. Apart from him, though, the house provides nothing by way of companionship, not even of the electronic kind—there is no television, of course, and cell-phone coverage is patchy at best. In the past, I used to take books along, but I've stopped now—I don't even enjoy the sound of someone else's voice in my head. Friends ask me, in genuine puzzlement, what I do with myself when I'm there. They think I'm being deliberately disingenuous when I tell them that I spend hours sitting on the porch, staring into the valley, and that I then switch to looking up at the sky for a similar duration, before I go for a long run. But that's honestly what I do!

I guess that's why, even though I came to swimming by chance, I took to it like, well, a fish to water, and stuck with it over the long haul. Swimming was solitary, it was demanding, it did not permit conversation. In fact, with my first coach, a traditionalist who was more heart than technique, all the sport asked of me was to 'Keep swimming!'. So I did, two hours every single day, all the way from ages ten to fifteen, and more when I was training for a tournament.

I want to digress briefly to make a point here. People use the words 'preparation' and 'training' interchangeably when it comes to sport, but, to me, there's actually a huge difference between the two. Preparation is something that happens over a long, long time; it is basic body-and-mind conditioning that you work at every single day, and it includes not just how much you exercise but also what you eat, how much you sleep and how you think. Training, on the other hand, is a burst of focused and intense activity over a short period to achieve some immediate goal. Training helps you 'win'. Preparation makes you who you are.

All those years of 'Keep swimming' were as much a part of my preparation as they were of my training. The other, more enjoyable, part of the prep was the wholesome, mildly spiced and absolutely delicious food Aai cooked each day. (To this day—she is eighty now—she has never let another cook enter her kitchen.) Those were simpler times—growing children were not recommended special diets packed with 'supplements' to make them tall or strong or healthy. Even those of us who were athletes were recommended nothing out of the ordinary. I remember drinking a lot of milk growing up, but that was only because I liked it so much. In fact, I eat far more vegetables today than I ever did as a child.

There is a lot of talk now about how Indian food is too rich in carbs and fat, how it is responsible for the Indian propensity for blocked arteries and heart disease, how vegan is the way to go and so on, but that, in my opinion, is nonsense—those arguments don't get to the root of the problem. We are less healthy today not because there's anything wrong with Indian food itself, but because of how we eat it. We now eat on a daily basis, or whenever the fancy takes us, the food we earlier only ate at celebrations. We constantly crave the exotic—different cuisines, different ways of treating food, a different grain that promises some wonderful health benefit—when all we need to do is stick to the simple, home-grown and familiar. Even today, with all the options open to me, I most often eat dal khichdi with lots of vegetables, whether I'm at home or travelling.

I firmly believe that when it comes down to it, good health is all about taking responsibility. Just like it is your responsibility not to be ignorant of the law, it is your responsibility not to be ignorant of your health. If you are truly mindful of what you put into your body every single day, if you take responsibility for keeping your body conditioned at all times, there is really nothing to worry about. It might seem bizarre, but I really don't know what a headache is or what a cold feels like. I fall ill so seldom that each episode stands out like a landmark event—two bouts of jaundice when I was younger, and a couple of run-ins with food poisoning in the more recent past, because I'm on the road so much. What's even crazier, my weight hasn't changed in thirty-five years—I weigh the same today— 80 kilos—as I did when I was nineteen!

You will notice I haven't mentioned keeping stress at bay as a factor for overall good health. There's a reason for that—I believe stress is a good thing. We would never get anything done if it wasn't for stress—all of humankind's progress has happened because we were dissatisfied with something and wanted to improve it to make our lives better. Why, hunger is a stress, thirst is a stress! So there's nothing wrong with stress—what we need to really think about is our reaction to it. Stress is a given—it is how you deal with it that defines who you are, and how you will live your life.

Swimming competitively at the national level was a huge stress. Training was an even bigger stress, and I did not enjoy it. But there was no way out—if I didn't train, I wouldn't, couldn't, win.

Once I had made my peace with that, that stress stopped affecting me in a negative way. Instead, it propelled me forward.

Baba added to the stress sometimes by seeing conspiracies where there were none, imputing favouritism to coaches, or ascribing my losses to 'politics'. He was constantly judging my fellow swimmers, insinuating that they were currying favour with the powers that be, insisting that they did not wish me well. In the end, I banned both my parents from attending any of my swimming events—Baba because of the reasons I've just listed, and Aai because, well, I was growing up, and no teenage boy likes being fussed over by his mom. At least in public.

~

'I'm young, I'm handsome, I'm fast, I'm pretty, and can't possibly be beat.'

—Muhammad Ali

At the age of fifteen, I suddenly began winning at the national level again. As I remember it, I won *everything*—every single junior tournament I competed in. What happens when you win consistently at the national level is that you get noticed. By the time I turned sixteen, I had been moved out of the care of my first coach and started training with coach Sandeep Divgikar. The venue changed too—I left my comfortable, laid-back public pool in Shivaji Park and started training at the by-membership-only Otters Club pool in Bandra. Once again, I was plunged, literally and figuratively, into a whole new world.

Swimming in India has always been an overwhelmingly urban and elitist sport, mainly because it calls for access to a pool. Most swimming pools, like the one at the Otters Club, for instance, were (and are) part of private clubs or fancy apartment complexes, so the demographic that took up swimming, even for leisure, was necessarily upper crust. The kids who trained at the Otters Club pool were no different. With my unfashionable buzz-cut, my glasses and my middle-class vibe, I stuck out like a sore thumb in their company; to them, I was above all the Marathi boy from Shivaji Park. The misfit was back.

Thinking back, I chuckle at how ironic it all was. In Shivaji Park, my mates had always thought of me as the 'posh' snob who read English books obsessively, spoke English with a foreign accent and did not know Marathi. In Bandra, it was quite the opposite—I was the hick from the boondocks who had to be humoured, if not pitied, the ingénue who had to be carefully educated on, say, what a typical teenage party in the burbs looked like.

I might have tried harder to belong to this beautiful set if training hadn't been so exhausting, so time-consuming. As it was, there was only enough time after training to rush back home and prepare for school the next day. Plus, while my parents were very proud of my achievements in the pool—Baba cut out and filed every newspaper clipping in which my name was mentioned—not everyone in the family approved of my desire to stick with competitive swimming after 10th grade. Four of my grandparents had been doctors, Baba was a scientist, Aai and my older sisters were teachers and academics—in such a family, a boy who did not pursue a 'proper'—read: professional—degree was bound to be frowned upon.

Context played a role as well, as it always does. My paternal grandfather had had a hard life—he had put himself through medical college both in India and England and, when he lost his first wife young, had married a lady doctor. With three young children from his first wife, the two of them had their hands full. But he made good, retiring as the Director of Haffkine Institute, the country's oldest and most premier research institute of tropical medicine. My grandmother, on her part, had been a professor at the J.J. Medical College in Mumbai for several years. My grandfather tried gently to dissuade me from a sporting career (in those days, an oxymoron at best). After all, he said, he had struggled so I may go further. The time for fun and games was over, he insisted; it was now time to get into academics seriously.

But I was loath to give it all up now, just when all the tireless years of preparation had begun to bear fruit. I had been told often by my coaches, and knew instinctively, that my best swimming years were ahead of me. Plus, I was fresh out of the three-month-long national swimming camp held before the 1982 Asian Games to pick the top swimmers to represent the country, where a world of hitherto unexplored possibilities had revealed themselves to me.

To be picked for the national camp was in itself an honour, but the part I had been completely unaware of was that all the participants would be training under a foreign coach, brought in expressly for the purpose of getting us tournament-ready. That year, the government had brought in a strict but brilliant East German coach. For the very first time since I had joined a coaching programme as a nine-year-old, I understood what a professional coach was all about and what a huge difference he could make to his wards' performance.

Indian swimmers lagged so far behind international standards that the coach did not even attempt to help us improve our timings. He simply focused on improving our body conditioning, correcting our stroke and technique and educating us on how we could, and should, enhance our daily prep. Training became a scientific, logical thing, very different from the 'Keep swimming' school of coaching. In what was an entirely novel experience, not only my body but also my brain was engaged in the process. I loved it.

I did not end up making the cut for the 1982 Asian Games, but I had never expected to. The guidance I had received under the East German coach, however, convinced me that I had so far only scratched the surface of my potential.

Now that I had been taught what to do to reach deeper, I knew I could make that great leap ahead. The 1986 Asian Games beckoned seductively—and my decision to stick with swimming was made.

To keep the family happy, I enrolled after 12th grade for a diploma in electrical engineering at Bombay's M.H. Saboo Siddik College of Engineering. The schedule was light, the courses undemanding—just the kind of support a boy who was planning to spend most of his time training needed. With a grand hope in my heart and stars in my eyes, I dived into the next stage of my swimming journey.

~

Two years is a long time, especially when you are training every morning and evening, swimming no less than 12 kilometres a day. In a 50-metre pool, 12 kilometres works out to 240 lengths. I am going to pause here for a moment and let you imagine it—all of us in training, stroking back and forth, back and forth across the pool, 240 times, every single day. In terms of time taken, it translated to close to five hours of daily swimming. At the end of each day, all we had the energy for was to crawl into bed and pass out. Just so that we could be up in time for training the next morning.

Such a rigorous schedule didn't leave me with much time for much else. Other kids my age were having the best time of their lives—hanging out with friends, going to the movies, eating out, bonding with girlfriends over late-night conversations. I, on the other hand, was, well, swimming. And swimming and swimming and swimming.

So yes, training was tough, but I don't remember resenting it too much. For routine, though much derided by the young and the restless, can be wonderfully calming—it centres you and gives you focus. You wake up each morning with purpose and fall asleep each night with a sense of accomplishment. In sport, the affirmation 'Every day and in every way, I'm getting better and better' ceases to be an abstraction; it becomes a quantifiable thing. When the figures tell you that you have indeed gotten better, you file it away as a good day and think no more of it, for today is now past, and tomorrow's challenge is already at hand. And when the figures tell you, as they often will, that you've slipped, you shrug and, once again, think no more of it—you know you can always try again the following day.

And so I continued training. I had known full well what the stakes were when I had willingly and voluntarily committed the next few years of my life to this grand project. Now I simply had to keep at it and see what happened.

What happened was this. In 1984, I was crowned the Indian Men's 100-metre breaststroke champion in the Open category. It was an incredible feeling for an eighteen-year-old. Until then, the gold had eluded me—there had always been two swimmers who had been faster, and I had been unable to get past the bronze. Now, for the first time, I was the undisputed champion—the fastest Indian man in the pool in the 100-metre breaststroke.

I was ecstatic. If I could manage to stay on top for the next two years, I could possibly represent India at the Seoul Asian Games in 1986. With that goal in mind, I went back to training with a vengeance.

I was the national champion in my category again the next year, and the next. I even represented India at the very first edition of the South Asian Games, which were held in Nepal the same year. The bigger thrill, though, was that I also set new state and national records for the event. Some of my records would stand, unchallenged, unbroken, for the next several years.

~

1986, the year of the Seoul Asian Games, finally rolled around. The list of swimmers that had been picked for the national swimming camp was announced, but I did not even need to check it—of course my name was going to be on it! This time, the government had retained an Australian coach, who was, by all accounts, even better and more cutting-edge in his training methods than the East German one. I showed up early on the first day of camp, eager to begin.

My excitement was rewarded almost instantly. The coach took one look at me in my swim gear and singled me out for special, more focused, training. 'You have the perfect swimmer's body,' he said simply. 'We can actually do something with this.'

I was stunned. Ever since I had begun to win at the national level, I had become used to being the cynosure of all eyes every time I stood on the starting block. I was used to seeing people nudge each other and mutter, 'That's the national champion!'

But I had begun to notice that people stared at *me* a lot more than they did at the other champion swimmers. I would have put their interest down to my 6-foot height, but many swimmers were just as tall. Plus, I had never thought of my height as particularly remarkable; it was entirely expected—everyone in my family was tall. What *was* it, then? I was beginning to have a strong suspicion that people looked so long and hard at me because of my—and I don't mean to brag here—*amazing* body.

How much of that body had been attained via nature and how much through nurture is moot, but at the risk of repeating myself, I was fully aware that, at age twenty-one, I had a truly spectacular physique. But to have a professional coach who had worked with some of the best swimmers in the world corroborate what I had merely suspected was a wildly different thing. The revelation that my body was not just beautifully sculpted but also superbly suited to what I was trying to accomplish blew my mind.

Maybe it also swelled my head a little. Maybe that's why I forgot, briefly, how things worked in the ego-ridden quagmire of insecurity that was the Swimming Federation of India back then. I forgot that officials often played favourites, picking brown-nosers over record holders for international tournaments, that they thrived on power play and that, ultimately, and most frustratingly, they held all the cards. Maybe it was that sudden delusion of invincibility that led me to ignore the little warning voice in my head, reminding me that swimmers weren't, by a long shot, the sports ministry's blue-eyed boys and girls—in fact, the officials saw us as snotty brats from cities like Bombay and Bangalore, almost always English-speaking, who did not hesitate to complain about the pathetic facilities accorded to athletes at sports camps or demand better conditions.

What increased their disdain for us was that unlike some of the track and field athletes and the hockey team, we hadn't the remotest chance of bringing home a medal, even at the Asian Games. If we were sent to international tournaments at all, the Federation constantly told us, we went on the sports ministry's sufferance and should therefore be grateful. In short, the ecosystem was not what one would call supportive.

It was against this background that I had my momentary, and regrettable, lapse of reason. The Indian national coach, incensed that I was giving his Aussie counterpart so much attention, began to insist, perversely, that I train as per his recommendations, that I ignore the instructions of the foreign coach. I was furious. It riled me that someone clearly less qualified and less experienced, at least as far as training champion swimmers went, would presume to come in the way of my progress. Looking straight at the Indian coach with all the arrogance a twenty-one-year-old national champion could muster, I said, loudly and clearly, 'Please don't interfere in my training. I prefer to do what this coach says, thank you very much.'

Retribution was swift and final. When the list of names of the Indian swimming contingent for the Seoul Games went up, mine was conspicuously absent. I was aghast. This could not be happening! How could they, how *dare* they, keep me, who had the most defensible reasons to be on the team, out of it? After all, I was not just the national record holder; I had also made the qualifying time for the Games! I demanded to know why I'd been dropped. The answer, when it came, would have been funny if it hadn't been so dystopian—I had been disqualified, they said, because my stroke was 'wrong'.

My stroke was *wrong*? My *stroke* was wrong? *My* stroke was wrong? It did not make sense, whichever way I looked at it. How come they had never noticed this huge failing then, in all my years of swimming and winning? Inside me, hot rage rose and boiled over like a river that had burst its banks. My infamous temper exploded. I had a huge showdown with the coach, and shot my mouth off once again—'It is because of people like you,' I raved, 'that Indian athletes will never get ahead.' He simply walked away, not even bothering to respond; secure in the knowledge that he had won this round, he didn't see why he should waste his breath. I was so angry I could have killed the man.

In the end, ironically, it was swimming itself that saved me from completely losing my mind. Over the years, swimming had become an outlet for my occasional bouts of violent adolescent temper—I had learnt that, however angry I was about something, I would be far less so after a two-hour training session at the pool. Swimming taught me how to put my anger away in a place where it would work *for* me instead of against me. It taught me to bide my time, to be infinitely patient, to trust that things would get better if I sat quietly back and let them.

For the next month, I continued to train at the camp, disbelieving, in denial. I sent off petitions to anyone whose word I believed could influence the composition of the team. I spoke several times to Suresh Kalmadi, the then sports minister of Maharashtra, begging him to take an interest. The Aussie coach personally sent a letter to the sports minister, Mrs Margaret Alva, making a case for me, asking her to see what she could do. But it was too little, too late. My Asian

Games dream fizzled and died before my very eyes, and there was absolutely nothing I could do about it.

Remarkably, though, my rage and gloom didn't put me off swimming. After the camp ended, I went right back to training. I won the national title again the next year, and the next, but it was all beginning to feel a little pointless, and my heart just wasn't in it any more.

But hey, I was still young (and handsome, and fast!). I told myself that it was time to shake off the nightmare of 1986 and head to fresh fields and pastures new. In 1988, at the age of twenty-three, I quit competitive swimming, never to return.

Things are much better for Indian sportspeople these days. In 2014, for the first time in the country's history, a true-blue sportsman, Olympic silver-medallist shooter Rajyavardhan Singh Rathore, was appointed minister for sports. There is now a board of Olympians that oversees the work of state sporting federations to make sure they are doing their job of spotting and grooming fresh talent. There are 'observers' for each sport—like Mary Kom, for boxing— who are also sportspeople, and they act as liaisons between the state federations and the central government. Although Rathore is no longer sports minister, 2019 is certainly a better time to be an Indian athlete than it was back then.

Although I never swam competitively again, I continue to enjoy swimming. I still have great conversations with my first coach, Percy Hakim, who I run into pretty regularly when I am home in Bombay. Whenever I meet Mr Kalmadi, as I do at various sporting events, we are nothing but cordial to each other. I don't know if he remembers my Asian Games debacle—I've never asked him, it doesn't matter to me. In that sense, I suppose I managed to put the whole hellish thing behind me pretty successfully and emerge, perhaps, more or less unscathed.

The thing is, when you are a sportsperson, winning and losing are such an integral part of the game, of your life, that you begin to view them somewhat differently from the way other people do. The line between what the world sees as 'success' and what it sees as 'failure' diminishes and disappears—you begin to see both simply as experiences that you can learn from, to truly become better and better. To be able to say 'I have never failed at things, only learnt from them' is to have truly attained a certain level of spiritual evolution, and if I say and feel that today—and I do—I can declare, hand on heart, that I learnt that particular lesson in the swimming pool.

Which is all good, and as it should be. But sometimes, when I look back, I think about what advice I would offer my haughty twenty-one-year-old self from my wise (well, *wiser*, anyway) fifty-four-year-old perch. The answer is unequivocal, and always the same. 'Dude,' I would say to him as he opened his mouth to let rip, 'shut the f*** up.'

KILOMETRE 23.2—BANDRA

6TH STANDARD CHARTERED MUMBAI MARATHON, SUNDAY, 18 JANUARY 2009

I ran through Shivaji Park, realizing with a start that, at 19 kilometres, I had gone right past one of the buildings of my Alma Mater, the Antonio Da Silva High School, within whose walls I had spent ten of the most formative years of my life, without giving it a second thought. But that wasn't entirely surprising—I'm the sort of person who, in a metaphorical sense, doesn't go back to where I've been.

When people ask me what my favourite place in the world is, the one city or beach or mountain I'd love to 'go back to', I have no answer. I have never felt the urge to return to a place simply because it held a happy memory. I rarely even revisit my past, whether with regret or longing, and I abhor standing still. My mantra, both in terms of living life and staying fit, is to

59

look ahead; it has always been encompassed in two words: Keep moving.

~

When I retired from competitive swimming, many people advised me to stay in the sport as a coach and mentor the next generation of champions. The idea did not appeal to me in the least, but I might have considered it if I hadn't found something else to do. As it turned out, I never had to, because a new career—modelling—landed, willy-nilly, in my lap. When the supermodel era ended, everyone wanted me to stick around in the industry—maybe I could start a talent-spotting agency, or mentor top models, or something? Once again, I demurred. In any case, I did not have the time; I was completely immersed in the next wave of opportunity, the next big thing—television.

The urge to keep moving, to not be held back by the endless what-ifs and what-might-have-beens, was true not just of my professional life. Each time I broke up with a girlfriend, there was always a sense of loss, to be sure, but seldom much regret—I believed implicitly that it was foolish to mourn something that had proved itself unsustainable in one way or another. Needless to say, not all my girlfriends saw it quite as I did, but each of us comes with our own karmic baggage and our own innate natures, and must therefore live our lives in different ways, reacting differently to the same situation—there is no way around that.

Essentially, I can't see myself as a teacher in the traditional sense, and I don't know how to be one. On the contrary, I have always seen myself as a lifelong student and learner, an explorer who follows the scent. And how do I learn? Simply by seeing everyone I engage with as a teacher. I am happy to be that kind of a teacher to whoever needs one. People are welcome to study my journey—the choices I've made and the consequences of those choices—and pick up whatever learnings they think they can use. They are even welcome to come along for the ride. But I cannot, will not, stop my own journey to hand-hold someone else—that would go against my nature and be fair to neither of us, for every individual needs to fashion his own unique path and walk down it alone.

As you can imagine, my beliefs are not designed to make me popular. In theory, they are easy to agree with; in practice, especially from those on the receiving end of them, there is often resentment, anger and bitterness. I have been told I am too cussed, too opinionated; I see it merely as having clarity about how I want to live my life. The wrangles with my dad turned me into someone who hates conflict and negativity and avoids both like the plague, so I never make a choice that will lead me into either, however pig-headed that choice may seem to someone else. I have been accused of being too independent, of not needing other people; I see it as being emotionally *self-sufficient, as feeling complete in oneself, and I highly recommend it.*

People say I am selfish, but isn't self-love the key to loving everyone and everything else? Self-love isn't narcissism—where the latter clouds your mind, seeing everything that is not 'me' as 'the other', inciting feelings of anger, hate and fear towards anyone who threatens what is 'mine'; instead, self-love dissolves imagined differences, operating on the principle of 'I'm ok, you're ok'. I hear that I have often been described as arrogant and egotistical; I believe strongly that it is those with small egos, which are weak and vulnerable and get bruised at every real and imagined slight, who create problems for the world. To have a giant ego is to embrace the universe and everything and everyone in it, to believe you are the universe—that large an ego is never in danger of being hurt and therefore incapable of, and completely uninterested in, wilfully causing hurt.

~

Past the halfway mark, at 21.3 kilometres—woohoo! This talking-to-myself thing was really helping take my mind off the heat! I was now just a little short of the Mahim Causeway, the narrow bridge across the smelly, sludge-filled, stagnant abomination that we Mumbaikars had turned the Mithi River into. Many residents don't even remember that the Mithi is a river until the monsoon hits and it swells and overflows its banks—*for most of the year, we know Mahim Causeway only as a frustrating traffic bottleneck. I had run this distance— the half-marathon—every year for the past five, and very comfortably, so I wasn't surprised that I was feeling good and running strongly. Of course, there were twenty-one more kilometres to go before I was back at the starting point, and the heat was really building up, but there was no sense in worrying about that now. Despite the niggling strain in my calf, I trusted my body—it hadn't let me down yet. Thus reassured, I returned to the absorbing task of reflecting on myself, and my motivations to 'keep moving'.*

While it was true that my credo was to be consistently forward-looking, that did not mean that I wanted to dissociate myself from the skills that I had spent so many years mastering, or the relationships I had taken so much joy in cultivating and nurturing; it did not, in any sense, involve a rejection of things that had gone before. In all the years since I had given up competitive swimming, I had never really stopped swimming— until running came along, it had remained my primary fitness activity. I had never really stopped modelling, either, or acting. I continued to be involved in both in bigger, if more tangential, ways—while I was still a model, I co-founded an event-management company (that also managed fashion shows), and while still acting in television, became partner in a production company. As for my once-girlfriends, I have remained good friends with many of them.

I like to keep moving for the simple reason that I am curious. To the curious person, the world is endlessly interesting, and he is loath to hang back, sticking only with what he knows. The new and unfamiliar does not intimidate him—he is willing to give even the most bizarre ideas a spin, to explore them with no preconceived notions, and no fear, simply because there is always some learning to be had at the end of each journey into the unknown. When you don't qualify the learning, when you don't tag it as 'good' or 'bad', or 'improving' or 'scarring', or 'worthy' or 'a waste of time', you will discover that any learning advances you in some way. What's not to like about that?

~

The pain in my calf was intruding into my thoughts now. To keep it at bay, I decided to quit the philosophical ruminations and think good, positive thoughts about my body, hoping like heck that that would help it heal.

I had learnt more things about my body since I had begun to run than I had in all my years as champion swimmer. I had started swimming when my body was still developing, and it had grown quite organically into a swimmer's body, fashioning itself into the most efficient shape and form for that sport. It wasn't at all that simple when I decided to become a runner at the age of thirty-seven. I had had to learn, consciously, how to move differently and how to use the same sets of muscles in new ways, so as to convert my body into one most suitable for running. It took time and it took patience, but because I had been a sportsman, it was easier for me than it might have been for someone who hadn't.

When you pursue a sport at a high level over a long period, some natural instincts get honed more than others, and certain neural pathways are enhanced. Like every other artiste whose art emphasizes physicality—dancers, gymnasts, Tai Chi practitioners, race-car drivers—I had developed a heightened sense of awareness of my body. I was constantly mindful of how it was moving, standing, resting, because being casual about my posture when I was sitting or falling asleep in a bad position could end up giving me a catch or a pulled muscle, and I could ill afford that as a competitive swimmer. I had also learnt to move 'efficiently'—to achieve maximum impact while causing minimum damage to my muscles and expending the least amount of energy. That instinctive awareness of the body, its balance, and how it moves in its environment is called 'proprioception', and I had it in spades.

It was my swimmer's body that got me an entry into modelling, but I believe it was my advanced sense of proprioception that helped me be successful at it—walking the ramp is all about arranging and moving your body in the most natural and efficient way—'like an animal'. For anyone watching, that kind of movement—that kind of natural confidence often called 'animal grace'—is also the most attractive thing in the world.

To this day, when I enter a room, people stop what they're doing to cop a look, either openly or covertly. Part of it could be because they know my face, but I like to think that a big part of it is simply the innate admiration we all feel for someone who occupies space in a 'natural' way.

I was past the Causeway now and on to the last straight, closing in on the 23.2-kilometre mark at the Bandra entrance of the Sea Link. This was the point at which the route doubled back on itself. Once I had gained it and made the U, it would lead me back to the starting point, past the same sights and streets I had come up along.

I had almost reached the U when it happened. Excruciating pain shot through my right calf as it tightened and seized. Cramp! No, no, no! This wasn't fair, this couldn't be right! I was barely 1 kilometre past the half-marathon distance and my first full was already in jeopardy. The heat and dehydration caused by all that sweating had caught up with me, and things were only going to go south hereon. With my talk of proprioception and the connection between my mind and my body, I had tempted the Fates to show me my place. I had been overconfident; I hadn't addressed the impending cramp until it had my calf in a vice.

Stop it! I told myself sternly. There is no doubt you overestimated your abilities, but moaning about that at this point is not going to help you. Focus on the goal! Force your mind to connect with your body now, *so that it can sweet-talk it all the way home.*

Right. With an effort, I hobbled to the U. 23.2 kilometres done in 2:09:43, 19.4 to go. I was still on course for my 3:45 finish. The cramp would slow me down for sure, but I could still hope for a sub-four-hour run, if nothing else went wrong. I mentally crossed my fingers. Keep moving!

3

RAMPING UP

'Its five-year mission: to explore strange new worlds . . . to boldly go where no man has gone before.'

—Capt. William Shatner of the Starship Enterprise,
Star Trek

Serendipity is my middle name. If there is one word I would choose, in hindsight, to explain the apparent twists and turns my life and career have taken, it would be that one.

When I emerged from the pool, figuratively speaking, at the age of twenty-three, the last years of the eighties were upon us. Looking around me with wide-open eyes for the first time in years, I noticed that something was changing, changing utterly, about the India of my childhood. You could smell it in the air, see it in the purposefulness on every face and feel it in the optimism with which people went about their business, even if you were never able to put your finger on what exactly the buzz was about. It was a strange and exhilarating time, and all of us who grew up in the seventies remember it—with a shiver of excitement—as that great inflection point in our country's life that matched one in our own.

Having completed my formal education and left competitive swimming behind, I now found myself at the proverbial crossroads. I had to decide, and quickly, what I wanted to do with the rest of my life, and think about how I proposed to earn my living. But as always, before I could begin to ponder this vitally important issue with the kind of seriousness it deserved, before I could draw up SWOT charts for various possible ways forward so that I could take a well-considered decision about my future, serendipity snuck in the door—a friend asked me to do him a favour. Since I had nothing better to do, I agreed, thus unwittingly setting course for a world so vastly removed from my own that I would not have found it even with the most sophisticated GPS.

With only the vaguest idea of what the word implied and what the profession entailed, I became a model.

~

It was my friend Bijoy Jain who was responsible for the whole thing. Bijoy and I had both been champion swimmers and had trained together for several years. At that point, Bijoy wanted to be a model, but ended up finding his mojo in architecture. He is a very well-known name in the field today, both at home and internationally, famous for designing and building airy, light-filled structures that are modernistic and traditional at the same time, from earth-based materials.

He would have made a great model too—Bijoy was and still is very good-looking. On the occasion I am referring to, he had in fact been contacted by Bombay model-coordinator Rasna Behl to audition for a print ad for Graviera Suitings. He could not make it to the audition for some reason, so he called and asked me if I would go in his place. I agreed and did the audition. A few days later, Rasna's team sent me their regrets. I looked too young to carry off a suit, they said, and for that reason, they had decided to go with someone else. I shrugged and carried on with my life.

That, really, should have been the end of that. But less than three weeks later, Rasna called again, saying that there was another opportunity—this time a shirting campaign for Thackersey Fabrics—which she thought I would be perfect for. I thought about it—did I really want to get into something I did not understand at all? Hell, yes!

All I would have to do, said Rasna, was wear some shirts and pose for photographs. The whole exercise, she reckoned, would take no longer than a couple of hours. And then she delivered the zinger: for this onerous, back-breaking act of physical labour, I would be paid—hold your breath!—50,000 rupees. Did that sound okay?

I was gobsmacked. Fifty thousand rupees is a lot of money even today, and this was thirty years ago, in 1989.

'When can we start?' I said.

When my face went up on the famous hoarding at Bombay's Cadbury House on Peddar Road a few weeks later, it was a really weird feeling—part embarrassment, part pride. Mostly, though, it was a relief, because it was something to show Aai. Ever since I had brought the fat cheque home, she had been very concerned, her fertile mind going over all the possible nefarious, criminal, immoral and/or downright wicked things her son could have done to come by that kind of money. This, at last, was irrefutable proof that I had been speaking the truth.

A few days after or before the Thackersey shoot—I can't remember now—Bijoy took me to a store called Ensemble, located in Bombay's Naval Dockyard area. I recall that he spoke excitedly about it—it was one of its kind, he said, a luxury clothing store and the first (and, at that time, only) multi-designer store in the city. It had been set up expressly to showcase the work of talented Indian 'fashion designers'. There were plans to host 'fashion shows' at the store, where models would walk up and down wearing Ensemble's clothes, showing them to a very special set of invitees. Seeing what the clothes looked like on real people would help the invitees decide what they wanted to buy for themselves. Pretty cool, huh?

I nodded, because that was what was expected of me, but I'm pretty sure my eyes were glazing over. This may seem ludicrous to someone born in the eighties and after, but I had no idea what he was going on about.

Bijoy told me that he was taking me to the store to meet two of its partners, who were both designers themselves—a Tarun Tahiliani and a Rohit Khosla. There was also going to be one other young and exciting designer there. He was looking for fresh faces to model his new menswear collection, and Bijoy thought I may have a chance. I shrugged and went along.

Once we were all introduced, the weirdest thing happened. The two partners and the other designer examined me critically with their eyes, from all angles, and then began to discuss me as if I wasn't even there. It was unsettling, to say the least, and, as I told myself then, discourteous to boot. They didn't notice my disapproval— they were too busy speaking animatedly with each other about if and how I could fit into the new, exciting and experimental thing they were trying. They were going to introduce India to 'haute couture', they exulted; they were going to change the way India dressed! They were bringing to our clothes an international aesthetic, a quirky vibe. We didn't have to be country cousins to the rest of the world any more—we would, if all went well, influence how the fashion-forward in other countries dressed in a few years' time!

Finally, they came to a decision. I would do very nicely as a model for that particular collection, they said, and asked me if I had any questions. What would the job pay, I asked, going all man-of-the-world on them. I had already done a shoot that had earned me 50,000, I was thinking, they would have to match that, surely, if they expected me to agree?

'Um,' the designer who wanted me said slowly, 'I'm sorry, but I cannot pay you, because I don't know if I'm going to make anything myself. The truth is, I have already invested all my money into creating this collection.'

I considered. The no-money thing was a bit of a bummer, and I did not 'get' these guys or their proposed business, but there was something about the mad glint in their eyes that appealed to me. They were all just a couple of years older than I, and they were trying to do something groundbreaking, something that hadn't been attempted before. However it ended, theirs was bound to be an interesting journey. If I rode shotgun, I would be assured of a ringside view. The explorer in me needed no further urging. Without further ado, we shook hands over the deal.

And that's how I got to model Rohit 'Gudda' Bal's first-ever menswear collection, and embarked on the wildest ride of my life.

~

Some context-setting is appropriate, even necessary, here. I have spoken earlier in this chapter of the optimism that was sweeping the country in the late eighties. It was only a low rumble then, but you could already see signs of how it would explode into a mighty roar over the next few years. A new generation of post-Independence Indians, untainted by the privations and traumas of their parents' generation, had come of age, in a decade when the world, bringing with it a host of never-before aspirations, had come into our living rooms via television. A young nation was breaking free of the shackles of dependency, revelling in its intact—nay, flourishing—democracy and gaining confidence by the day.

Our scattered but significant successes in the sporting arena were one big reason for that upsurge in confidence. At the beginning of the decade, in 1980, a soft-spoken, mild-mannered young man from Bangalore had become the first Indian to win the All-England Open Badminton Championships, dethroning the legendary reigning champion, Indonesia's Liem Swie King, with his lightning-fast wristwork. His name was Prakash Padukone. The same year, in the Moscow Olympics, the Indian men's hockey team regained the gold after a sixteen-year drought. Given that so many top hockey-playing countries had boycotted that edition of the Olympics, the medal was missing some of its sheen, but it still went some way in making the team, and us, feel better about ourselves.

Two years later, New Delhi played host to thirty-three countries at the 1982 Asian Games, in the process transforming itself into an international city of world-class stadia and cutting-edge transport and telecommunication infrastructure. Flyovers made their appearance for the first time in the country, and the state-owned television channel, Doordarshan, geared up for its first-ever live broadcast as every middle-class household in our sports-mad nation scrambled to get itself a television set; it was unthinkable not to be a part of the Games.

India finished fifth in the medals tally, and a young girl from Kerala called P.T. Usha won the silver in the 100-metre and 200-metre sprints, snagging her country's attention for the first time. At the Olympics two years later, she would miss a podium finish by a whisker, but would return in triumph from her next Asian Games outing in 1986 (yup, the same one I so cruelly lost the chance to be a part of) with a haul of four golds and a silver, changing how the world—and India—perceived Indian female athletes.

In 1983, one of the most enduring, heart-swelling memories of the decade was created when the Indian cricket team, against whom the London bookies had offered 50:1 odds at the beginning of the tournament, lifted the Cricket World Cup for the first time. That win created an even bigger following—if such a thing was possible in a country whose majority religion was already cricket—for the sport, culminating in the kind of financial and cultural superiority the BCCI enjoys in the world today. In 1988, the quiet genius of Chennai lad Viswanathan Anand won him the title of India's first grandmaster, setting him on course to become one of the world's greatest chess players. In 1989, a sixteen-year-old cricket prodigy called Sachin Tendulkar made his international Test debut, setting the crease—and our collective imagination—on fire.

There were other things besides sports to celebrate as well, particularly the propitious beginnings of journeys that would find full expression in the coming decades. Notwithstanding a tumultuous ten years in our political and economic life—which saw the near secession of one of our most prosperous states, the assassination of a popular prime minister and a devastating industrial disaster, often characterized as the world's worst, in which over 2000 people perished in their beds on a cold December night from inhaling poisonous gas that had leaked out of an American pesticide plant in the city of Bhopal—several affirming events in our country's history also came to pass.

In 1984, the first Indian astronaut, Squadron Leader Rakesh Sharma, orbited the earth and returned to tell the tale. Our first indigenously developed long-range nuclear missile, Agni, was successfully test-fired, creating nervous ripples from Washington to Beijing. The Maruti 800, India's most beloved, most influential, family car, was rolled out, ushering in our consumer revolution. The first bona fide multinational IT firm, Texas Instruments, set up shop in Bangalore, even as homegrown IT major Infosys Technologies began its operations out of a one-bedroom apartment in Pune. And the vision of a young, new prime minister, who had his country's mandate firmly behind him, saw our telecommunications programme take a huge leap forward.

But perhaps the most momentous change the decade had wrought in the lives of common people was how we spent our evenings (and Sunday mornings!). Television had every Indian family in its thrall, and the fact that there was only one channel ensured that the whole country watched the exact same programmes. The stupendous, record-breaking success of Ramanand Sagar's *Ramayan* and B.R. Chopra's *Mahabharat* proved that, even at the fag end of the twentieth century, it was mythology that got us going. But other original series did tremendously well too—it was one of them, *Fauji*, that catapulted a young Shah Rukh Khan directly off television screens and into Indian hearts.

Bollywood, the other great religion of India, was changing too. The decade had been one of the bleakest in Bollywood history, but it had redeemed itself at the last minute with the 1988 sleeper hit *Qayamat Se Qayamat Tak*. *QSQT* took the film-going public by storm, launched the careers of actor Aamir Khan, playback singers Udit Narayan and Alka Yagnik and debutante director Mansoor Khan, established Juhi Chawla as the nation's most beloved girl-you-could-take-home-to-mom and proved conclusively that the era of the angry young man was finally over.

All these disparate indications that the country was on the cusp of momentous change converged to their natural culmination when, pushed to the wall by a huge financial crisis in 1990, the government decided to (finally!) introduce major economic reforms and allow foreign companies to come in. Liberalization opened the floodgates like never before, accelerating the Indian economy, creating the world's biggest middle-class—which brought in its wake a never-before consumer boom—and taking us, boldly and jubilantly, where no Indian had gone before.

Phew. That tale was long in the telling.

But the story is important, for it was against the backdrop of this churn that the Indian fashion industry was born. My family and I had missed the whole television revolution—as

I mentioned in a previous chapter, Baba had given away our television set on our return to India—but I would go on to become one of the defining faces of the fashion revolution.

It was pretty ironic, coming to think of it, that fate would choose me for this. Particularly because—surprise, surprise!—I have always detested being photographed.

~

It was a strange, strange world that I entered into, in the Bombay of 1989. Nothing in my solid middle-class upbringing or my years as a champion sportsman had prepared me for the people I met in the nascent world of Indian fashion. The designers whose work Ensemble carried—Rohit Khosla, Rohit Bal, Abu Jani–Sandeep Khosla and Tarun Tahiliani himself—were among the pioneers of the industry, but to me, they all seemed more than a little mad. Well, weird, anyway, and as different from me as could be possible.

For one thing, unlike me, most designers came from very wealthy business families. For another, they were almost all part of Delhi's swish set, which had a completely different culture to Bombay's. They worked hard, sure, but they partied harder, and their live-on-the-edge-and-experiment-with-everything lifestyles came as an eye-popping revelation to a boy who had never had so much as alcohol pass his lips because his parents frowned on it and because he had been a sportsman-in-training all his adult life. Many of them experimented with their sexualities, and some were quite openly gay.

But perhaps what made these and other designers most exotic in my eyes were the things they spoke so passionately about—aesthetic, cut, weave, design, texture, silhouette, and always, always, that most ubiquitous and desperately vital thing, *style*. Their preoccupation with clothes, shoes and accessories, and with how things *looked* and *felt*, far more than how useful or functional they were, was alien to me— even the women in my life were nowhere near as obsessed with beauty and structure and form as these men were.

These days, I am often asked about the 'casting couch' in the fashion industry, back in the days when I was a model. So many gay designers with access to so many beautiful boys—surely there was plenty of action? The truth is, while that may or may not be true today, it certainly wasn't the case then. The industry was in its infancy, and it was all very innocent, very idealistic, populated by a bunch of dreamers with hopes and ideas and ambition, having fun while they figured out how to make their fortunes. Plus, the designers were very young; not one was a big name yet, with the power to make or break a model's career. In fact, *they* were the ones scouting for models to show their clothes, not the other way around. It was all very different, as you can see, from how it is today.

For me, the best thing about being part of this set was that, despite our differences, we got on like a house on fire. My designer friends could be wacky, wild and totally over the top, but I could see that they were also hugely talented. For someone like me, who is eternally curious, it was a great learning experience simply to be around them, watching them work and listening to their conversations. I settled happily into the gilded opulence of this new world of make-believe that I had wandered into, and waited, all senses at the ready, for the new adventures it would bring.

~

'It's not safe out here. It's wondrous, with treasures to satiate desires both subtle and gross. But it's not for the timid.'

—Q, in the episode 'Q Who?', *Star Trek*, Season 2

If you have read this far, you have probably guessed that I am more than a little obsessive by nature. When I went through my reading phase as a child, I read obsessively—finishing an entire series before moving on immediately and seamlessly to the next. As a swimmer, I swam so obsessively that I couldn't stop for two years *after* I had been cheated out of what had been a lifelong goal. Modelling was no different.

My modelling years—the five years between 1989 and 1994 when I did most of my work—were an intense, heady time. Bombay's high society had invited Ensemble into its heart and was clamouring for more, while the Indian middle-class, which had only ever had its clothes 'designed' and stitched by the neighbourhood *darzi*, looked on from the sidelines, fascinated. My fellow models, like me, almost always came from the other side of the velvet ropes, but we were still somewhat elite—our convent-school backgrounds, our exposure to Western ideas (through the books we read and the movies we watched) and our felicity for spoken English gave us an edge over other young people our age. Top that off with good looks, fine clothes, a hedonistic lifestyle and a lot of money (I used to earn something like Rs 35,000 per show), all beamed out to a hungry nation via television, and you have stirred up a potent and seductive cocktail.

The media fell madly in love with that image of us. We made it to every magazine cover, every weekend newspaper supplement. (As I have already mentioned, I did not enjoy being photographed, which is why I did very few print ads in my time, saving all my energy and exposure for the ramp, but, to the media at least, I quickly learnt to give the impression that I did—the whole charade demanded it.) We were interviewed and quoted all the time, and objectified endlessly. Before we knew it, some of us—Mehr Jessia, Madhu Sapre and I, to name just three—had been anointed 'supermodels'.

Given the fact that most journalists who covered the fashion/lifestyle beat were young women (is there any other kind? To this day, all journalists who ever interview me seem to be young women), I got more attention, which translated into rather more column inches than I strictly deserved. It made some of the other male models a little insecure—'Why is he such a darling of the media?' was a constant murmur in the background.

I can only guess at the reasons. I certainly wasn't the only good-looking one—in fact, I was less buff and darker-skinned than most, so it wasn't that. I did not go out of my way to schmooze with the right people or promote myself—I did not care enough—so it wasn't that either. Maybe it was just that my general enthusiasm for very many different things made me a more interesting subject to journalists—I could (and often did) have freewheeling conversations with them about much more than fashion and the modelling life. Maybe it was that I understood, subconsciously, what a newsworthy 'sound bite' was long before it was a thing, and provided those. Whatever it was, it worked. Readers lapped it all up and gave me more love than I knew what to do with.

It was all a bit overwhelming in the beginning, to be honest, but I got used to it in a bit. I got used to girls calling my name wherever I went, kissing my hands, wanting to touch me. To my friends from a different lifetime, however, my dizzying rise to celebrityhood was completely bewildering. I remember—was it in 1994?—walking into a lounge in Pune one night with a close friend from college who had returned home for the holidays from his university in the US. He knew that I was a model, and a decently successful one at that, and that my pictures often made it to the magazines, but he had not, in his wildest dreams, guessed at how that played out in real life. The moment we walked into the club, all the girls there began to scream, just *scream*. The poor guy was in shock for a while after.

And it wasn't just the screaming either. I have never understood this thing about fandom, where the fans literally want a piece of you, but the fetish is universal, and truer for celebrities in glamour, entertainment and sport. Speaking for myself, I have never liked to sequester myself in a VIP area or surround myself with security personnel—that kind of thing would compromise my own sense of freedom too much and deny me the opportunity of living a normal life. But there are times when I have wondered if a little isolation may not be such a bad idea.

And that's why, sometimes, despite acknowledging and appreciating all the advantages of having such a recognizable face, I end up feeling just a little cheated. It would be interesting, I can't help feeling, to have a more *real* life, to not have to question every relationship, or wonder each time what someone *really* wants from me. One of the unfortunate fallouts of my stardom is that the restricted social interaction it imposes is even less than what a happy loner like me would have wished for.

The flip side, though, the weird part, is that fans feel that they know the (apparently inaccessible) object of their adoration really well. People come up to me all the time and speak to me like I am their friend, and get offended if I don't respond in a similar fashion. That doesn't just mean that they expect me to be warm, it also means that I can say anything I like to them—even nasty, offensive, patronizing stuff—in an affectionate, humorous way, and they genuinely won't mind! We are complete strangers to each other, but they will accept from me, indulgently, the kind of comments that they would not tolerate from anyone except their best friends and family. When you think about it, it's all a little bizarre.

But whenever I feel like it is all getting a bit much, I only have to think back to the time when I first met the great Amitabh Bachchan. One of the perks of celebrityhood is that you get to meet other, bigger, celebrities and superstars you have heard about and admired your whole life, and it was no different for me. It happened at the height of my modelling career, when I had gotten used to thinking of myself as a pretty big cheese. One night, I was at the nightclub at the Taj in Colaba, when my friend, the well-known Bombay socialite (now, after her own bout with cancer, she is a formidable cancer activist and counsellor) Devika Bhojwani popped in and asked me to join her and 'some friends' for dinner at one of the restaurants. I swaggered in a little while later, and found that 'some friends' included Mr Bachchan himself!

I went weak in the knees. With a spectacular lack of compunction and moderation, I unleashed my inner fanboy all over him. I must have come across as terribly gauche. But he was so gracious that whenever I think back to that day, I only feel warm and fuzzy, never embarrassed. If such a big star could do that for a relative unknown like me, surely, I tell myself, I can do the same for people who consider me worthy of their fandom.

And that's why, as far as possible, I try to keep my interactions with people, with fans, as real as I possibly can. Over the years, I have become more self-aware and learnt the little trick of observing myself as I interact with others. I am now able to call myself out the moment I start to cross my self-imposed boundaries of good behaviour—when I'm about to retort with an unnecessary barb, say, or poke fun at someone—even when I know it won't be taken badly.

I use this trick not just with fans but also in my professional interactions—where earlier I used to cut in when a potential client, partner or employee was speaking, and *tell* him where I thought he was going with an argument, and why he was wrong, I have learnt to listen quietly until he finishes his piece, and *then* give him my point of view. It's a small thing, but it makes a world of a difference to the other person—everybody deserves a respectful hearing.

The heightened self-awareness has worked remarkably well for me. People often tell me today that they are pleasantly surprised at how down-to-earth I am, how non-celebrity-like. But really, I'm just being me. It's just that because of the above-average number of interactions I am involved in on a daily basis—often with complete strangers—and the slightly unreal quality of the life I lead, I have been forced to become a little more reflective than I might otherwise have been. That has helped me hold on to my true identity—that of a shy, middle-class Marathi boy from Shivaji Park—versus my manufactured one—supermodel/Ironman/ladykiller. That makes me very proud indeed.

Come to think of it, in a funny, roundabout way, it is my very celebrityhood that has ended up grounding me, and put me on the path to some of life's great lessons—patience, acceptance, detachment and self-control.

~

I have spoken earlier of the alcohol and banned substances that were such a staple in the fashion scene. Factor in the social acceptability of such a lifestyle within that particular echo chamber—in fact, *not* indulging marked you out for a weirdo—the ease of access, the parties you were obliged to attend as part of 'networking', the fact that I was flush with funds and my obsessive streak, and you have a potentially dangerous situation on your hands. My inveterate need to experiment, to try everything new and exciting and unfamiliar at least once, nudged things along nicely. Before long, even though, hand on heart, I didn't even really enjoy the taste of it very much, I was knocking back a great deal of alcohol every night and enjoying my occasional line (or two) of Charlie.

There was another development that accelerated my journey to alcohol overload. In 1989, around the time when I first started hanging out with Bombay's fashionable set, I began dating a fascinating girl many years older than I. Like my designer friends, she also came from a wealthy family and cared deeply about things that I was completely clueless about—music, dance, art, culture. She had also been involved in helping organize a bunch of high-profile events, including the extravaganza—some of you may remember it—that was the Yves St Laurent fashion show, part of the 150th birthday celebrations of the 'old lady of Bori Bunder', the *Times of India*. The Festival of France was also being celebrated that year, and the whole of the bay—from the skyscraper-ed splendour of Nariman Point to the sands of Chowpatty along Marine Drive—had been transformed into one seamless amphitheatre, a grand canvas to showcase France's technological achievements.

The fashion show itself was dazzling; the thought of it still gives me goosebumps. It happened at the Gateway of India, I remember, and the ramp entry was designed so as to make the audience feel as if the models were emerging, à la Ursula Andress in *Dr. No*, from the Arabian Sea itself. The fact that we cannot dream of such an event happening today, in our fraught, high-security, post-26/11 world, is, for me, one of the most poignant indications of how irrevocably the world has changed.

I think what I loved most about the girl I was dating was her energy and her efficiency. I also admired her for all the things she knew and was touched that she was so willing to teach them to me. So when she proposed that we went into business together, I agreed instantly. And that's how I became an entrepreneur at the age of twenty-three, as 50 per cent partner in what was one of India's first professional event-management companies.

My first adventure in event management was all kinds of exciting, and our company got to plan, design and execute some seriously exclusive events. One that sticks in my memory dates back to the beautiful evening in 1990 that was artist M.F. Husain's seventy-fifth birthday party. The other is that of a more long-term assignment, which we took on for well-known Bombay hotelier Ravi Ghai. As you will see, this one was significant for quite another reason.

In 1991, Ravi Ghai launched the eponymous RG's, a fancy new restaurant-cum-nightclub-cum-discotheque, at the famous Hotel Nataraj on Marine Drive. The dance floor was sunken, the DJ had been trained in London and there was a never-before 'video wall' to boot. It was an exclusive club, with membership capped at 300. As you can imagine, that got Bombay's young and happening all buzzed, and RG's became very popular very quickly. Unfortunately, after a stabbing incident one night, it dropped out of favour just as quickly. Keen to restore its cool image, the hotel hired us to create unusual, attention-grabbing events, and one of the ideas I came up with was celebrity bartending nights. Three nights a week, we'd get a Bombay celebrity to come in and take charge of the bar, hoping that having them there would not only attract their own crowd but also those that would show up just to see and be seen with the celebrity.

My job on each of those nights was to stand at the door, offering everyone who walked in free shots of vodka to get them excited. I don't know whose idea it was originally, but by and by, a twist was added to this little ceremony—if the customer did a shot, I would do one as well. It became something of a draw, and I thrived on the attention, revelling in my own machismo at not keeling over even after downing more shots than was sensible by any stretch of the imagination. It became so bad that I was doing (at least) an entire bottle of vodka, straight, three nights a week, apart from all the recreational drinking I was doing before and around that. I would stumble home, smashed out of my skull, each Wednesday, Friday and Saturday night for months, unmindful of Aai's complete disapproval and utter disgust. I think she hardly spoke to me during those months, but to her credit, she didn't make my life at home unpleasant in any other way.

The drugs were another story. I didn't do the dirty stuff— LSD, Ecstasy, heroin—preferring instead to stick to my favourites, marijuana and coke. Luckily, I never got addicted to either, for two reasons: I was never really fond of them (although I did enjoy how hyper I got after a Charlie fix), and I still had 'sportsman's hangover'—I believed implicitly that anything that was detrimental to overall fitness was a very bad idea. For me, doing drugs was just a way of participating in the action. When it's just lying around and everyone around you is doing it so casually, all the time, it's easy to forget, at least temporarily, your other life—the one in which this stuff is considered so bad (and with good reason!) that people don't even speak of it except in disapproving euphemisms.

The other reason I kept doing it was that the drugs didn't affect me all that much. I was still able to do what I had to do, personally and professionally, when I was under the influence. Until that one time in Pune, in 1994, at a fashion show towards the fag end of my modelling career, when someone, annoyed that smoking two joints had apparently had no effect on me, gave me a piece of hash to chew. I chewed it up and, still insisting that '*nothing* is happening', went off to my room to relax before the show. An hour or two later, my eyelids fluttered open. I knew instantly that something was very wrong. I could hear the programme on the television and I could see the screen, but I couldn't see the figures moving—they seemed to be frozen. My head was spinning like a top, and when I tried to get up, my limbs refused to cooperate. Oh-*kay*, I remember thinking to myself, so *this* is what actually happens to you when you do drugs.

Since there was nothing else I could do, I decided to lie back and give myself up to the experience. My friends arrived to check on me a while later, concerned that I hadn't turned up to get dressed for the show. When I did not respond to their insistent knocking, they went away and came back with the hotel manager and got the door opened. They were pretty rattled at my state of immobility, but I still had enough control over my senses to indicate to them that I was okay and would just have to wait until the effects of the hash had passed.

I did not do that show in the end—I couldn't. It was very unprofessional of me, and it took me a while to get over the guilt. But it was just the wake-up call (haha!) that I needed, and I gave them up completely. As for the alcohol, I still enjoy a very occasional drink, at an office party for instance (okay, maybe I did get quite smashed on bhang a couple of years ago, after a very, very long time). But the regular binge-drinking stopped entirely after my modelling years.

Yup, just like that.

So even though that probably makes me very boring, I do not have an Alcoholics Anonymous or life-in-rehab story to tell, despite the excesses of those years. Perhaps it was because, in my case, neither alcohol nor drugs were an escape from anything; they were just youthful high jinks, a delayed adolescence to make up for all the years consumed by rigorous sports training. Plus, I still lived with my mother in my parents' home, where access to alcohol was non-existent. Most importantly, my self-esteem, usually the first thing to take a beating when one is in the throes of an addiction, continued to be rock-solid. (How come? I attribute it partly to my nature, partly to the detachment I learnt to feel for success and failure during my swimming years and partly to a mother who always had my back.)

The thing is, I have never believed in 'mind over matter'. I believe it's really mind over mind—the body is a poor slave that, as long as it is properly and lovingly nourished, has no sense of its own agency; it will simply do what the mind tells it to. At the end of those (literally) intoxicating, intoxicated years, my mind decided that while the abuse had been 'fun', after a fashion, it was now quite enough. And that, really, was the end of that.

Until I started acting in television and began to smoke obsessively. Nature can be a b***h like that.

~

'Set phasers to stun.'

—Order often issued by officers on the Starship
Enterprise, *Star Trek*

One of the many milestone moments in the Indian fashion and glamour industry in the eighties and early nineties was the opening of the very first National Institute of Fashion Technology (NIFT) in New Delhi in 1986, which ensured a steady flow of new and exciting young designers, gung-ho about Indian textiles and weaves and full of edgy ideas about cut and drape, into the market. The other was the crowning of a twenty-one-year-old Indian girl as the second runner-up at the Miss Universe pageant in 1992. It was the first time since 1970, when Zeenat Aman had been crowned Miss Asia-Pacific, that an Indian had placed among the top three at any international beauty pageant.

But her podium finish at Miss Universe wasn't the only reason Madhu Sapre made such a huge ripple in the popular consciousness or left such a lasting impression on it. In fact, it was her conscious and unconscious flouting of all kinds of norms, both societal and institutional, that made her a hero. Her unconventional looks—Madhu was too tall, too dark-skinned, too slim and too angular to fit the traditional Indian ideal of feminine beauty—did not deter her, for instance, from participating in a beauty contest (the Femina Miss India pageant). When she won it, she changed the country's perception—and the perception of legions of dark-skinned girls like herself—of beauty itself.

When she scored an almost-perfect 9.9 out of 10 in the swimsuit round at Miss Universe, the highest ever by an Indian contestant, organizers of the Miss India pageant took note, and included a swimsuit round (horror of horrors—Indian girls baring so much skin!) in the Indian edition. Two years later, this addition, along with several other suggestions made by Madhu after her Miss Universe experience, would see two better-prepared Indian contestants—Sushmita Sen and Aishwarya Rai—clinch both the Miss Universe and Miss World crowns in a landmark outing.

And then, of course, there was her (in)famous response to the final question at the Miss Universe pageant. Unlike most other female models of the time, Madhu had built her statuesque, perfectly toned body on the sports field—she had been a national-level volleyball player before she began to model. And therefore, when she was asked, in the pageant's title-decider round, 'What would you do for your country if you were prime minister?', she answered, unhesitatingly and truthfully, that she would build a world-class sports complex, so that other girls would not have to suffer like she had from having to use inferior sporting facilities. That politically incorrect 'gaffe' (the 'correct' answer would have been something far more noble-sounding—and completely infeasible—like 'I will do my best to eradicate poverty') not only cost her the crown but also brought the whole country's disdain upon her for being such a clueless hick. But Madhu was unfazed; today, her conviction about what the country really needed is borne out by an entire generation of world-beating Indian sportswomen who have had access to precisely such first-class facilities.

Right. All this elaborate scene-setting was simply to establish that Madhu was already a national celebrity by the time I met her later the same year. People think that we were drawn to each other because of our backgrounds—we were both from Bombay, both Maharashtrian, both sportspeople. The truth is that I fell in love with Madhu Sapre simply because she was such a sweet, unspoilt person, so comfortable in her own skin. Within the fashion fraternity, she was even more of an outlier than I was, in one key aspect—English was not her strong suit; when she did speak it, it was with a thick Marathi accent. In India, and within a certain set, that kind of handicap can be severely debilitating to one's self-esteem. But even that did not come in the way of the goals Madhu set for herself and, with her strong work ethic and unwavering focus, achieved.

By the time we met, the media had already followed, tracked and love-hated the two of us as individuals. When we became a couple, we were pitched into a whole new orbit of media gaga. Madhu–Milind, in short, spelt Magic.

Luckily, our professional rise mirrored each other's. Towards the end of 1992, Madhu, Mehr and I received an invitation from a British modelling agency to come and try our luck there. Mehr hated the London scene and returned home pretty quickly. But Madhu and I stuck it out for almost two years, although Madhu was far less comfortable away from India than I was. (The funny part is that she has lived in Italy for almost two decades now, while I, since then, have never lived outside India.)

London was anything but a holiday. When we did have work, the schedules were punishing, when we didn't, which was often—it was really not a good time for exotic models—we were out on the streets, knocking on doors, auditioning for places in shows, looking for work. Like I said, Madhu did not enjoy it all that much, but for me, it was exhilarating beyond belief. This was supposedly a world I had belonged to for the last three years, but the European version of that world was vastly, fantastically different from anything I had ever seen. I ended up spending a year each in London and in Paris, and experienced the unbeatable joy of having my mind blown wide open, again.

I mean, think about it. Here were the world's greatest, most iconic, designers—thought leaders whose word and work decided the trends that the entire world would follow—and here *I* was (if only briefly) with a golden ticket to legitimately access them, their designs and their studios. Just looking at their clothes, and being able to feel them and wear them and see how beautifully they fit, was a privilege— and a revelation.

Luckily for me, this was a time when India was inspiring designers from New York to Paris, and mehndi, nose rings, anklets, sequinned embroidery, beaded evening wear and churidars/jodhpurs were on runways everywhere—so I had some reference points. I got to see exactly how a *bandhgala*, for instance, conceived and designed by a Karl Lagerfeld or an Oscar de la Renta or an Armani or an Yves St Laurent was different from one designed by an Indian designer. Because a completely ethnic Indian look would never fly on an international runway, these designers used Indian fabrics and colours sparingly, elegantly and very, very creatively— the silhouette was Indian, and some bits, maybe the inside of a cuff or a collar, would use an Indian fabric, but the way the jacket was cut and styled made it a garment that would not look out of place in any international setting. The tailoring, the finish and the drape were near perfect—those bandhgalas were, simply, the best in the world.

The imaginativeness these designers displayed in the storytelling they used in their ramp shows and the edginess of the styling that even small boutique photographers brought to their fashion photography were seriously eye-opening. I cannot pretend I understood how gigantic nose-rings and anklets went with lingerie or leather jackets, but if you kept an open mind, a glimmer of understanding would sometimes filter through.

And then—those goosebumps again!—there was the London Fashion Week and the Paris Fashion Week. I spent all the money I made in those years to make sure I attended those events, if only as a part of the audience, because the experience was so spectacular. I cannot ever forget the thrill, the absolute wonder, of walking up and down the Champs-Élysées during Paris Fashion Week and staring wide-eyed and open-mouthed at the thousands, literally *thousands*, of the most beautiful humans on the planet—sitting at pavement bistros, lounging in the parks, strolling aimlessly, seeing and being seen. And these were the aspirants, mind you, the ones who had *not* made it to the top bracket—the *real* models were elsewhere, away from the hoi polloi.

The sensory overload and the alienness of all the things I experienced during my two years abroad was the equivalent of putting my brain through a giant washing machine where someone had forgotten to separate the whites and coloureds—my mind came out cleaner, free of the encrusted grime of years of preconceived notions and tempered with a multitude of hues from all the other perspectives it had been sloshing around with; all of which turned it way more interesting, and way less judgemental, than before.

The exposure to some of the world's most talented people in my industry also successfully diminished, *demolished*, my sense of importance in my own eyes. And just for that, I am eternally grateful.

~

1995 was a very significant year for me in many, many ways.

In January that year, my father died, leaving me with a bunch of mixed feelings to sort through, but not much grief. I had never had a great deal of affection for him, which is rather sad when you come to think of it, because he cared deeply for me in his own way. When he had moved out of home five years before he died, I remember feeling nothing but a huge sense of relief; as I sat by his prone form in the ambulance that was taking him to the hospital, I tried to muster up some warm emotion for him, but did not succeed.

It was the end of an important and not always happy chapter in my life; fortunately for me, I was able to make my peace with it sooner rather than later.

Right on the heels of my father's passing came the music video. Yup, *that* video. The one that single-handedly propelled the singer—the pint-sized, sweet-faced, 'baby doll' Alisha Chinai—into the stratosphere of musical fame. And turned me from a supermodel into something way bigger—a star.

But first, there are a couple of clarifications/disclaimers I want to issue:

- In a video that is 4 minutes 19 seconds long, I'm on-screen for a mere 53 seconds, give or take a couple.
- When the song was first played to me and the concept of the video explained, I thought it was unbelievably tacky, and I didn't shy away from airing my unsolicited opinion to director Ken Ghosh and Alisha herself. They went ahead and made it anyway.

Let me jog your memory a bit here, so that you can decide for yourself if I was right or wrong about the 'tacky' part. 'Made in India'—the song around which the music video was made—tells the story of the lovely

Alisha, the princess of the land of Yashab. Alisha (played by the eponymous singer herself) is looking for her perfect mate—a dreamboat who will capture her heart and sweep her off her feet. She has travelled the world seeking him, and has had her pick of the finest specimens of every race—Mongoloid, Negroid, Caucasian—but none of them has been able to get her adrenalin pumping, and her feet have remained resolutely on the ground. At her wit's end, she takes herself to a sorcerer of some kind ('exotic India' stereotypes, anyone? There are snakes and a snake charmer in the video as well, and an elephant, a pet leopard, a dancing sadhu, a Kathakali dancer and a guy doing yoga—no, seriously!) who conjures up, out of a fog in a copper basin, the image of a well-muscled—in a nice way—Indian man. Alisha is smitten but has no idea where she can find this man of her dreams. She takes to moping sadly on her throne, until . . .

You can guess the rest. One fine day, the copper-basin guy arrives in her court—cringe alert!—packed inside a wooden crate stamped with the words 'Made in India'. Unboxed by his attendants, he climbs out, bare-chested and dhoti-clad, picks up the besotted princess and carries her away to their 'happily ever after'. Urggghhh.

Needless to say, yours truly played the eye candy. I finished shooting my part in less than half a day and went on to my next assignment, convinced that the video would at best air a few times and then sink like a stone. As it turned out, I was quite, quite off the mark.

'Made in India'—both the song and the album—became a monster hit. It sold, according to industry reports, a staggering five million copies in India and abroad; single-handedly established the genre called Indipop; and catapulted Alisha into the position of its reigning queen. It was also the first homegrown pop album to give Hindi film music a serious run for its money.

I have often wondered about the factors that were responsible for this. And I always come back to the same three things—timing, timing and television. It was 1995, only four years after liberalization, and the mood in the country was unbelievably upbeat. A new confidence was swelling the hearts of Indians of every stripe, and the dominant emotion could be summed up in a phrase that would not be coined until much later—*Mera Bharat Mahan*.

'Made in India' captured the zeitgeist like nothing else. Not just Indian products, Alisha was saying, but Indian *people*, Indian *men*, were the most desirable in the world. Naturally, India roared in approval.

Television—read: Channel V—played its part too. Smart, hip, homegrown Channel V, created in 1994 expressly to fill the 'youth channel' vacuum left by the retreating American behemoth MTV, which simply could not find its feet in this market in its first outing, was the perfect setting for

'Made in India'. In direct contrast to MTV, Channel V had a decidedly Indian soul and used a mix of irreverence, self-deprecating humour and Hinglish to serve up never-before music programming in a genre that did not exist before they invented it—'desi cool'.

In addition, the casting was perfect. To choose a dark-skinned model to play the princess's paramour was a master stroke. It sent out a powerful message: after years of grovelling before the West, first as part of our colonial hangover and then as part of a phenomenon we named the 'brain drain', where our brightest and best fled the shores for the blandishments of America, we were finally getting comfortable in our own (dark) skin.

I was cast in several other music videos after that, including two with Alisha herself, but while some of them caught the imagination of the viewers—like 'Jaanam Samjha Karo', sung by Asha Bhosle and composed by Leslie Lewis, featuring Helen Brodie and me in the lead; the 'Aa Jaane Jaan' remix with Shenaz Treasurywala; 'Yeh Wadiyan' with Jeanne Michael; and Sonu Nigam's 'Is Kadar Pyaar Hai' with Michelle Innes—none of them came close to the wild popularity of 'Made in India'.

And I had thought it was tacky. Clearly, my tastes were out of sync with everyone else's. If I needed one more shout-out from the universe to let me know that I was a misfit, this was it.

It was also a very clear signal that my lucky star was alive and well, and still looking out for me.

~

When life hands you an exhilarating high, you can bet that she will soon blindside you with an excruciating low. It's nothing personal—she does it simply to keep things interesting. And so it was with me. Unfortunately for her, Madhu was also involved in this one, and the blowback was much harsher for her than it was for me.

Yup, I'm talking now of the ad. *That* ad. The one in which the admen, in their wisdom, put the two of us in a tight clinch without a stitch between us and assured us breezily that everyone's attention would be on the sneakers we were advertising (brand name Tuff), and not us. Oh, they also put a python in there somewhere. This was still 1995.

But first, full disclosure—this was not my first photo shoot in the buff. A couple of years earlier, I was doing a photo shoot for designer Suneet Varma at the Ridge in Delhi, with photographer Bharat Sikka in attendance. After we had completed the shoot, Bharat said he would like to attempt some nude photography with me if I was okay with it. I have always been very comfortable with my body, so I simply dropped my clothes and posed for him. There were other people around—we could hear them—but the Ridge is a large, wooded space, and we managed successfully to stay concealed.

The pictures—which were really quite beautiful—were offered to the Bombay edition of the *Saturday Times* (this was the weekend supplement of the *Times of India* then, before each city got its own daily supplement), which prudishly refused to publish them. Very surprisingly, the Delhi edition, which I had always expected to be more conservative, agreed to publish them, and did. The pictures, which became the toast of the town, raised not a single murmur of protest.

The Tuff shoes print ad, however, was quite another story. When Ashok Kurien and Elsie Nanji of Ambience Advertising approached Madhu and me with the proposal, we both agreed almost immediately. It helped that the two of us were seeing each other in real life, but even if we hadn't been dating, I don't think either of us would have had too many reservations; Madhu was just as comfortable with her body as I was with mine. We were even more reassured by the fact that one of India's finest fashion and fine-art photographers, Prabuddha Dasgupta, was going to be shooting the campaign.

The actual shoot passed off without incident. We were told that the July editions of *Cine Blitz* and *G* (tagline: Glamour, Glory and Grandeur) were going to carry the ad.

Satisfied, the two of us went back to work and thought no more of it.

Cut to the first week of July. The magazines had been up on the stands for no more than a few hours when all hell broke loose. Word of the ad had got out to some of the more conservative political parties, and they reacted with the kind of lightning speed and efficiency that I haven't seen before or since. Coming down hard on the managements of the magazines, they demanded that every single copy of the July issue be pulled from circulation. The magazines complied, and we breathed again, believing the worst was over.

On 23 July, the *Sunday Mid-day* ran a story on the clampdown and used an image of the controversial ad in it. That was when the shit really hit the fan. People who knew of the story but had not seen the ad now got to see it. Before we knew it, women's organizations were protesting outside Madhu's house against her lack of 'culture', burning copies of *Cine Blitz* and handing her father stacks of saris. Since his daughter was apparently too poor to afford her own, they explained, and her parents too irresponsible to provide her with a few, they had decided to make a donation.

In early August, a public interest litigation was filed against all the accused—the producers and distributors of the magazines that had carried the ad, the advertising agency, the photographer, the director of Tuff shoes and the two of us—for obscenity. Soon after, another case was brought against Ambience under the Wildlife Protection Act, for the illegal use of a python, accusing the agency of cruelty to animals. Both cases would drag on for fourteen years before all charges were finally dismissed.

I never discussed my work at home, so Aai was completely taken by surprise when the furore broke out. But she wisely refrained from commenting on it; her concern was entirely for Madhu, whom she was very fond of. In any case, neither Aai nor I had to face the kind of public ire that Madhu's family did. Luckily, Madhu had told her parents about the campaign and had even shown them the photograph before it was published. Her mum had been disapproving, but her dad had been very cool, even going so far as to say that it was a very nice photograph. Through the entire ruckus, he stood by her like a rock.

But the whole episode was very tough on Madhu. On the one hand, she blamed herself for doing something that had caused her parents to be hounded and harassed. On the other, she herself had to deal with a whole lot of trouble— the unkindest cut being that her passport was confiscated for a while, cutting off all her foreign travel, whether for work or leisure, for over a year.

It was all patently unfair—I didn't have my passport taken away, nor was I harassed half as much—and it exposed the hypocrisy of patriarchal societies in a way that made me sick to the stomach. But apart from standing by Madhu, there was nothing I could do.

The case was finally resolved in November 2009, a full fourteen years after it had been filed, with the court dismissing all charges against all the accused. Madhu and I had split up a long time before that happened, in 1998—we had different plans for our lives. But everything we had been through together kept us close—we remain friends to this day.

KILOMETRE 32.5—WORLI SEA FACE

6TH STANDARD CHARTERED MUMBAI MARATHON, SUNDAY, 18 JANUARY 2009

26 kilometres. I was still going, and going quite well, in fact, for someone with a cramp. But fear had begun to cloud my mind now, fear that the course was far from done, fear that more cramps were on the way, fear that the heat would—but of course it would!—get more intense, fear that if, when, those things happened, I would have to give up. Somehow, I had to block out the fear.

I wished I was the sort of person who could get lost in music, who could get so absorbed in a particularly sublime bass line or rhythm pattern that he could forget everything else around him. But I am one of those rare weirdos who isn't interested in music, any music—I have no playlists on my phone; I never have music playing in my car or in my home.

Two more painful kilometres done, and the fear had begun to turn to irritation, to anger. I had prepared well for this race. I had bided my time, running the half for five years before attempting the full. In those five years, I had run 10 kilometres at least three times a week, apart from longer runs a couple of times a month. All that physical activity ensured that my body burned up anything I ate like it was a joke. Even so, in the last three months, preparing for this big one, I had cut back on the hamburgers and chocolate that I loved so much, replacing them with vegetarian protein, which I knew was a cleaner protein— the body expended much less energy burning vegetarian calories, leaving more over for other activities, like running. It had been a huge sacrifice. I had not cheated on myself in any way—I had made every day in training count. I had completed two 30-kilometre runs in the last month, petering the training off over the last couple of weeks until I had entirely stopped four days ago, to allow my body to rest completely, so that it could make its maiden assault in the best fettle.

But to what end? All my training had been to ensure that I could not only run a marathon, but also run it comfortably, yet I had been let down in the 22nd kilometre itself! If I had attempted the full the very next year after I had completed my first half, without any of the training I'd done in the past five years, the result may not have been any different.

This was what came of believing that what worked for other people would work for me, I thought, furious with myself.

I knew my body, and I should have trusted my own gut more. What misguided fool had decided that one should never run the full course in practice? How did that even make sense? Didn't common logic dictate that if one was attempting the 42k, one should run 45k in training, not 30? Just so that you believed wholeheartedly, and whole-mindedly, that you could do it, because you had already done it before? How had I, who was such a passionate advocate of mind over mind, not have seen such a basic truth? The mind, in any case, was a monkey, jumping from one thought to another constantly, using up 25 per cent of the body's energy on a given day. Surely, I should have realized that giving it one more thing to worry about—Can I actually run 42k? No, you can't. Oh yes, I can! How can you be so sure? You've never done it before—would be most unwise. Instead of helping my body conserve energy and divert it to where it was really needed, I had actively plotted to do the opposite!

I was overheating in every way—physically, mentally, emotionally—as I re-entered Shivaji Park. As always, just being in these beloved environs stoked the embers of memory and brought a measure of peace. I wondered how many miles Baba had covered while walking these streets—he had always been a great one for walking. I thought about Aai, the fittest sixty-nine-year-old I knew, who was now a member of a club that went out on one trek a month. My sisters and I, all strong swimmers, had benefited so much by taking our fitness cues from the example our parents had set for us.

By now, I was past the 28-kilometre mark and about half a kilometre short of the Siddhivinayak Temple. It struck me that I was coming up to the 18-mile mark, the dreaded distance at which the body runs out of all its reserves of energy and hits the seemingly insurmountable barrier that long-distance runners call 'The Wall'. I checked my watch—I had been running for about three hours now. Science had discovered that the human body can do any sustained physical activity, like running, at a certain intensity, for a period of three to three-and-a-half hours, quite naturally—to be able to run beyond that is what you train for. I had trained plenty, not just in the past few months but through my entire life, but my mind would not let me forget that I had never actually run beyond 30 kilometres at a stretch. Something awful was coming. I knew it.

Right on cue, without any warning at all, and with all the warnings in the world, my left calf muscle seized up. The pain was unbelievable. I was in agony. This time, however, I was at an advantage over the cramp—instead of the shock and disbelief that had stunned me when the first one hit, there was only a grim joy that what I had dreaded so much had actually happened. The catastrophe was no longer impending—it was here. Fear disappeared. Come at me, cramp!

I plodded on down Annie Besant Road, both calves out of commission, the 10 a.m. sun blazing down on my head,* *taking*

---

* What a blessing that the amateur full marathon now has a start time of 5.30 a.m. (instead of the 6.45 a.m. it was then)!

heart from those runners around me who looked even worse off—misery, as everyone knows, loves company. The atmosphere was festive by now, with far more people outside their homes, lining the streets, cheering, than there had been on the way up. 'Captain Vyom!' a young voice called out from the crowd, in sudden, delighted recognition. 'Hero!'

I turned my head to see if I could spot him, but sweat was pouring into my eyes, and everything was a blur of colour and noise. With an effort, I raised my hand in the general direction of the voice, in grateful acknowledgement. When I was feeling least like one, someone had called me a hero. Sure, it was a fictional hero he was invoking, a character I'd played in a TV series in the nineties, but for now, it was enough to give me a fresh spurt of energy, a second wind.

Right on to R.G. Thadani Marg, and back on to Worli Sea Face, expecting nothing but more pain and more rebellion from my beleaguered body. When it came, about halfway down the Sea Face, it showed up as excruciating pain in my quadriceps— at 32.5k, throwing up their hands at my pig-headed insistence to keep running, the muscles in my thighs had seized, joining the general mutiny.

32.5k done, 3 hours 12 minutes gone. Stunningly, I had kept up a decent pace through my calf cramps, but there was no way I could keep going at that speed any longer. I had exactly 10 kilometres to go, and it would be a bloody miracle if I could simply stay upright and keep moving.

4

SCREEN TIME

'The director sent for me for Tarzan. I climbed the tree and walked out on a limb. The next day, I was told I was an actor.'

—Johnny Weissmuller, five-time Olympic gold-medallist swimmer and actor known for his iconic role as Tarzan, in *Tarzan the Ape Man*

While 'Made in India' was the 'acting' assignment that was responsible for making me 'go viral', it was by no means my first one. The same year—yup, we're still in 1995—a landmark TV series was launched on the state-owned television channel, Doordarshan. It was India's first English series—have we had any since?—from a time when television was brave, experimental and fresh, when it did not concern itself solely with mythological sagas, or worse, conniving mothers- and daughters-in-law. The series had a catchy and memorable title track, and it was called, rather poetically, *A Mouthful of Sky*. I played one of the lead characters.

But *Mouthful* wasn't my first casting call. In 1990, a full five years before this series hit the screens, a young moviemaker who had directed the blockbuster film I mentioned earlier—*Qayamat Se Qayamat Tak*—had come calling. He had a role for me, he said, in his upcoming film, tentatively titled *Jo Jeeta Wohi Sikandar*. He had seen me on the cover of *GFQ* (Gentleman's Fashion Quarterly), liked my 'intensity' and thought I would be perfect for the negative male lead, Shekhar Malhotra.

I was stunned. This was Mansoor Khan, who had already delivered, on his debut, what would become one of the most talked-about films in Bollywood history!

It would have been foolish to reject Mansoor's offer, so I didn't. But the excitement I felt about the project was not so much about the possibility of becoming an actor as it was about trying something new, something different, that had fallen into my lap as serendipitously as things always seemed to do. I mean, I didn't even speak Hindi at any level of fluency then! As for my acting experience, although I had done a bit of elocution and drama at school, and even been good at it, I had always naturally been happier with my books than under the arc lights.

My excitement, however, was tinged with misgivings, especially in one respect. You see, in those days, all of us models thought ourselves quite superior to Hindi film actors and actresses. We were the beautiful people, all sophisticated and English-speaking, who dressed according to global fashion trends, knew not only posture and walk but also fine food and wine, and understood how to wear clothes and style them (it was amazing how quickly the Marathi boy from Shivaji Park, who had known absolutely nothing about drape and design just a couple of years before, had morphed into this). To our condescending eyes, Hindi actors seemed loud and crass and bling-ed out—their sense of humour (at least on-screen) never rising beyond slapstick, their dancing moves bawdy when they weren't plain ridiculous. And as for their acting—well, the less said about that hammy, melodramatic and exaggerated thing that went by that name, the better.

That was what we said to ourselves, anyway, in the cosy echo-chamber of privilege that we occupied in the golden years of modelling. We killed ourselves laughing at the absurd costumes that huge stars like Madhuri Dixit, Karisma Kapoor, Sridevi and Urmila Matondkar wore in the movies of that time, swearing that these women had to be the worst-dressed in the world. (Before you judge us too harshly, put this book down and pull up, on your computer, some of the iconic movies of the late eighties and nineties starring

these actors. Now watch them, even just the songs—and
then tell me, hand on heart, if their clothes don't make you
cringe a little.)

One particular incident sticks out in my mind. It must
have been in 1991–92, and a bunch of us models were
returning from a show in south Bombay. At the Haji Ali
Juice Centre, we made our regular stop for a late-night
milkshake—for those not in the know, that was, and is, a
very Bombay thing to do. As we waited for our order to be
served, a jeep pulled up in front of us and Shah Rukh Khan
jumped out, along with a few others that I didn't recognize.
He ordered his milkshake and, in the next moment, climbed
on to the roof of the jeep and began dancing to the song
blaring out of its stereo (he was clearly very excited about
something; maybe he had just signed his first film—either
way, that man has always had more energy than he knows
what to do with). A crowd gathered quickly and began
to cheer him on—he was already the hugely popular and
much-beloved star of *Fauji* then. We, on the other hand,
were cringing so hard that we got quickly back into our
cabs and drove away. Like I said, we really thought we were
something pretty special.

But Mansoor Khan was not your run-of-the-mill
Bollywood person. For one, he came from a completely
different background, traversing a huge arc of academic
achievement—IIT, Cornell and, as if that wasn't enough,

MIT as well—before he chose to veer off that path and pursue a career in Hindi cinema. He brought to his film-making all kinds of new perspectives—and a lovely restraint—from his years abroad, while keeping the emotions themselves very Indian. In *QSQT*, he had taken a pretty hackneyed Romeo–Juliet plot and presented it in such a fresh, heart-rending way, bringing in an almost entirely new cast (which included, of course, his nephew Aamir Khan, in his debut film), that it had left both stick-in-the-mud conservatives and young liberals gutted, and gushing.

I was sure he would do something equally exciting with *Jo Jeeta Wohi Sikandar*, and he did—*JJWS* became a megahit too. Unfortunately, though, I lasted only as long as the first shooting schedule. I quit for a reason that I am quite certain will never make it to the list of 'Top 10 Reasons Why People Quit Films'—I quit because the crew did not feed me enough.

No, seriously.

You must remember that this was still 1990—I had just come off being a full-time swimmer, a sportsman in training. For several years, I had lived by a very strict routine that included, apart from the discipline of 'early to bed and early to rise', a LOT of food. Even among my fellow swimmers, my appetite was legendary. It was quite routine for me to polish off, at breakfast alone, a whole loaf of bread with an entire 100-gram pack of Amul butter, along with a quarter kilo of chocolate and a giant portion of daliya. At training camp, I was the one who picked up the entire serving bowl of whatever had been served for breakfast, after everyone had left the table, and licked it clean. That would be followed up with a modest ten rotis with dal and sabzi at lunch, at least four sandwiches at teatime and another ten rotis at dinner. And this was apart from the bananas, fried eggs and the two glasses of milk that were a daily staple.

On the sets of *JJWS*, that routine was shot to hell. If you recall, a bicycle race was one of the core plot points of the film, and all the 'kids' in the film cycled everywhere. So there I was, take after take, cycling up and down the hills of Ooty and Kodaikanal, returning to base completely exhausted when filming was done, *only to find that there was no food*! For some incomprehensible reason, it would dawn on the crew that we might need to eat only when they saw us arrive, at which point someone would say, 'So shall we get some biryani?' That biryani would take a long time to be delivered, by which time it would be stone cold, not to mention unnecessarily greasy and spicy. That was usually the point at which my famous temper, always at the ready, would explode. I remember creating major scenes—throwing my bicycle to the ground, kicking it around, cursing. To be honest, I don't know how the other actors managed, but they seemed to do quite well on fresh air and cigarettes.

Either way, by the end of the first shooting schedule, I had had enough, and quit.

Mansoor held auditions for the role again—Akshay Kumar had been one of the hopefuls—but eventually cast Deepak Tijori in the role. As for me, I was so put off with the meal culture—or the lack of it, more accurately—in Bollywood that I didn't return to it until ten years later, for my own debut, in *Tarkieb*.

Did I ever regret not sticking with *JJWS*, especially after it became such a big hit? Not really. I had never wanted to be an actor in the first place—as I mentioned before, I had a very supercilious attitude towards the movies—and in my other life as a model, I was at the top of my game and had more work than I could handle. I was more concerned that I had behaved so badly on set, although it had never happened in full public view, and was hoping that would not affect my relationship with Mansoor, who I had taken a genuine shine to. Luckily for me, it did not seem to—I ended up sitting next to him at the premiere, and he was as cordial and warm as he had ever been.

My outbursts of anger had begun to concern me, though. I was beginning to see a lot of Baba in me, and I didn't like it at all. I knew I needed to find a way to rein it in, if only to prove to myself that I did indeed have the ability to do it. Sure, I could have hidden behind the excuse that it was my father's fault really, because I had my father's genes, but

I have never been able to be anything but brutally honest with myself. Baba's anger was basically the result of a low threshold of tolerance to situations where things did not go as he believed they should, and my rational mind told me that was a silly way to live—seriously, how much control does one really have over things outside of oneself? It was my responsibility as a thinking, intelligent adult to fashion my own response to such triggers, instead of taking the lazy way out and taking a cue from his.

I understood all this at an intellectual level, but it would be many years before I succeeded in putting any of it into practice. It was only when I went back to sport, long-distance running this time, that I was able to convert any mental and emotional stress that I had into physical stress and let it flow out in the most natural, least damaging way.

Don't ask my co-workers and partners at the various foundations and business enterprises I am involved in about this calm, tranquil Milind, though—they will deny he exists. I still rage around the office and yell a lot when people take their responsibilities lightly, or fail to demonstrate commitment. That kind of visible anger is often required to make people understand the kind of work ethic I expect them to bring to their jobs, to make them believe that I'm not a pushover. What has changed is that I am now able to unleash this anger mindfully; when something annoys me, I am able to step back, review the situation and decide whether a yelling is required; the situation itself does not force my hand.

More importantly, this premeditated anger (even if the premeditation has only lasted thirty seconds) does not hurt me; it has a purpose, and once that purpose has been achieved, I am free to get back to my day, and even to my interactions with the person I've just yelled at—with no baggage. Oh, and mindful anger has another great fallout— it releases some of the stress that has built up inside you without your knowledge, as a result of the daily irritants of city living (traffic, a surly cab driver, potholes, a new and ugly hoarding) at regular intervals, thus preventing the stress from bursting out of you at inopportune times or killing you from the inside out.

It's a wonderful thing—this being able to watch yourself be passionate, in a dispassionate manner; it isn't easy to learn the art, but now that I am some part of the way there, I am a big fan.

~

But back to *Mouthful*. In 1995, my friend Devika Bhojwani (remember her? I had fanboy-ed over Amitabh Bachchan at a dinner she was hosting?) was working with Plus Channel, a company that created content for radio and television, apart from full-fledged feature films. They were toying with the idea of creating India's first English TV series, and once they had roped in Mahesh Bhatt as director and novelist Ashok Banker as sole scriptwriter, they were ready to roll.

Devika urged me to audition for it, dangling the big fat carrot of 'It's in English!' in front of my nose. I resisted, because I had just received an offer from Amol Palekar for the role of a transvestite in his new film *Daayra*, and I wanted very much to do it.

A male supermodel, at the peak of his career, eager to essay the role of a transvestite in his film debut? I'll admit it isn't common, and almost everyone I knew advised me strongly against it, but the delicious irony of it was precisely what made the idea of it more interesting to me. I have always been as much a gay pin-up as a woman's fantasy—in fact, the Tuff ad was talked about by the Indian gay community as being as much an iconic moment in their history as it was in Indian heteronormative history. The fact that I had been surrounded by gay men in the fashion industry—many of them were clearly attracted to me, but never made a move, bless them—had often led me to wonder about the nature of sexuality.

Come to think of it, I had wondered about it for much longer than that. I was only twelve or thirteen when I realized that the older boys who chased me around the swimming pool had something more than just play in mind—one of them even kissed me in the changing room when I was around fourteen or fifteen, while the others stood by, laughing and clapping. Even though I had been pretty cocooned in my small world of home, school and pool—I heard the word 'sexy' being spoken (and not with respect to me, either) for the first time only after I had turned sixteen—the kiss didn't feel like sexual abuse, perhaps because there was nothing clandestine or threatening about it at all. Luckily, I had no confusion about my own sexuality, so I grew up pretty unscarred, even flattered, by all the male attention.

That attention persists to this day—in 2006, I was tickled to discover that an Indian film-maker in America called Harjant Gill had made a short documentary about notions of home and belonging among gay South Asians who are part of the diaspora, called *Milind Soman Made Me Gay*! (You can catch it on YouTube any time, but I must add a disclaimer here—I feature only in the title). Speculation about my sexuality, and my sexual morals, persist in the public imagination, though—there is this story that has been doing the rounds for many years, about me being the main squeeze of a very eminent—and single—industrial magnate; apparently, I travel with him in his private jet every time he goes off on vacation. I am very amused by this particular story, especially because I have never even met the man. (It makes great business sense for me to do so soon, though. I would love to partner with one of his companies to create an event or a campaign around something related to women's health and fitness; when I do get around to it, maybe I will tell him this story and we can have a quiet chuckle over it.)

Right. Where were we before this necessary digression? Ah, yes, *Daayra*. Well, that film was taking its own time to get on the floors, so when Devika asked me again to audition for *Mouthful* a couple of months later, I agreed, thinking that shooting for a series would give me an opportunity to hone whatever acting chops I might possess, so that I would be better prepared for *Daayra*. (I was expectedly nervous about shooting with someone like Amol Palekar, given that I had no real acting experience at all.) The audition went well, Mahesh was pleased, and before I knew it, I had landed my first role in a television series. Unfortunately, by the time Amol was ready to begin shooting *Daayra*, he had changed his mind about me and instead cast Nirmal Pandey in the role. Bit of a shame, that—I would have loved to play that role, and experience, if only vicariously, the life of a transvestite.

Luckily, *Mouthful*, which was a story from the 'I-Know-What-You-Did-Last-Summer' slasher-thriller genre, went on to do very well. The story revolved around five friends, all MBAs, who reunite thirteen years after they have graduated, to collectively face a macabre secret from their past which is threatening to destroy their present. The initial excitement about it, apart from the fact that it was in English, was that the cast was full of models—there was Samir Soni, Ranjeev

Mulchandani, Parvin Dabas, Neesha Singh, Kamal Sidhu and myself—apart from fresh debutant actors like Rahul Bose, R. Madhavan and Simone Singh (who, as we all know, went on to become well-known names after). Doordarshan gave the show a late-night slot because of its 'adult' content. We rolled our eyes about that then, but in retrospect, DD's decision seems sensible and right, especially in the light of what passes for wholesome 'family' content on primetime TV these days.

Mouthful's five leads—named Prithvi, Pavan, Akash (who I played) and so on, after the five elements—represented different aspects of the new generation of post-Independence urban Indians struggling to reconcile their Indian and Westernized selves. That part resonated so much with my own experience—in many ways, Akash (he was connected to books too, being an author) was me—that shooting for the series, even though it was pretty rigorous—we shot twenty days a month for a whole year and produced 252 thirty-minute episodes in all—ended up being very enjoyable indeed.

Even though it was critically panned in India, *Mouthful* was shown in some thirty-odd countries, which was a strong enough stamp of approval for the series as far as I was concerned. It got me noticed as an actor too, although not always in a good way. If I remember correctly, 'wooden' was the adjective most often used to describe my (apparently non-existent) acting skills. That kind of negative feedback could have put someone off acting for life, but I didn't let it bother me too much. I reasoned that just like swimming or singing, one got better at acting through practice. If I expected to be hailed as a brilliant actor in my very first series, I told myself, especially when I had never wanted to be an actor at all, I was being an idiot. Secondly, directors were calling me all the time, offering me roles—if I had been such a terrible actor, they wouldn't be doing that, surely?

Thirdly, and most importantly, *mere paas maa thi*. Aai thought I was good in the series, and she, as you know, does not dispense compliments often or lightly. (Okay, maybe she didn't *actually* say that in so many words, but at least she didn't say I was wooden, and that was enough for me.) And Aai got to watch me play Akash because . . . Yup, on the morning of the day that *Mouthful* aired for the first time, I made sure that a brand-new television set was delivered at our doorstep. For the first time in over twenty years, and well after my dad and all three of my sisters had left home, Aai had something she could amuse herself with in the evenings when she got back from work.

Ultimately, though, and to my own mind, my real takeaway from *Mouthful* was not better acting chops. Simply by being a part of the series, I had learnt so much about how content was produced for television that by the very next year, I had partnered with film-maker Parvati Balagopalan to float a film- and television-production company called E-Motion Pictures. This is how it happened.

Sometime in 1996, either when *Mouthful* was winding down or after I had begun shooting for my next TV series, *Sea Hawks*, Parvati came to see me. She had her own company then, called Parvati Pictures, and she had an idea for a TV series in which she wanted me to play the lead. The love story was set in 1965, she said, and would play out in Goa, against the backdrop of its liberation from the Portuguese by the Indian Armed Forces. It would have twenty-six episodes, it would be, erm, a *Hindi* series, and it was tentatively called *Margarita*.

Something about the story—looking back, I think it might have been the fact that like me, Pedro and his girl, Margarita, straddled two worlds, Indian and European—grabbed me from the word go. I wasn't content to be just acting in it, either; my inner control freak wanted to produce it too, to ensure that it would turn out exactly as I wanted it to. I was even willing to take Hindi lessons!

I asked Parvati what she thought about me coming in as a partner in her film-production company. She went away and chewed on the idea for a bit, and came back saying she had nothing against it in principle; she would be quite happy to have me on board. We discussed the details, drew up the contracts and went into business as E-Motion Pictures in 1997. So yes, that's how I fashioned my next shiny, happy hat—after being swimmer, model, entrepreneur and actor, I was now a film producer. In that sense, I suppose I cannot wash my hands of all responsibility for where I am today, or attribute it entirely to serendipity. It was serendipity that dangled an opportunity before me, sure, but it was the active choice I made to grab it that really made the difference.

In my experience, the grabbing of the opportunity itself is often an impulsive decision, at least for me—I decide to chase something simply because I think it could be interesting—but it is what comes after that really makes the magic happen, and that is what you really commit to when you make your decision. You commit to putting in the tedious, frustrating work that every learning curve involves. You commit to taking some very real risks—in the case of E-Motion, I ran the risk of losing a lot of money if a movie tanked or a series wasn't commissioned. You commit to dealing with spectacular failure, of which there is always a very good chance, especially when you venture into something you have no previous experience with.

The advantage a control freak like me has when he gets into something new is that if he ends up with egg on his face, he will only have himself to blame for it. That knowledge can be scary to some people, but to me, it is very comforting—I hate failing at something because someone *else* did not do something that he or she should have. Also, as I tell myself each time I step into unexplored territory, there's no way of knowing for sure that I will fail at something until I have tried it, is there?

~

'Space, the final frontier.'

—The first line of every *Star Trek* episode, spoken
by Captain Kirk

The television years continued. As Commandant Vikram Rajpoot, I was part of the much-loved *Sea Hawks*, based on the lives of the officers of the Indian Coast Guard. It was a riveting action drama, and the only Indian TV series that was shot on land, water and underwater. *Sea Hawks* remained India's no. 1 TV show for the entire year that it aired, and turned R. Madhavan, who played Deputy Commandant Preet, into the nation's lover boy.

There was another series—based entirely on legal eagles—called *Vakaalat*, in which I shared screen time with Rahul Bose and Mini Mathur, and another one called *Tanha*, which never made it to TV. In hindsight, though, all of these, even *Mouthful*, seem only training grounds, mere trailers, to the one breakout series that fulfilled my own childhood dream of playing an intergalactic superhero and introduced me to a new generation of Indians. At 10 a.m. each Sunday morning, starting in late 1998 and continuing well into 1999, legions of Indian children gathered around their television sets to cheer their favourite superhero in his mission to capture twelve of the most dreaded supervillains in the universe. They didn't know (and cared not a whit) that I had once been supermodel Milind Soman; they only knew me—and loved me—as Captain Vyom.

Set in the year 2123, when humans have become the masters of the solar system, *Captain Vyom* was a landmark series on many counts—as I write this, I realize how often the word landmark has come up while describing my television years. If *Mouthful* was landmark for being the only English series and *Sea Hawks* for being the only action-adventure filmed on land and sea, *Vyom* was the first futuristic sci-fi series on Indian TV. It was directed by the brilliant Ketan Mehta, and cost three times as much to produce as any other series, simply because at least ten of the thirty minutes of each episode was taken up with special effects, all of which were created by Ketan's own SFX company, Maya the Magic Shop.

Some of the elements of the overall plot that still stand out for me are these: the 'World Government' is headquartered not in New York but New Delhi; the oldest and wisest being in the solar system is not Master Oogway, who lives in China, but Astro Guru, who lives on Mars (Astro Guru thought up solutions to the world's problems using a potent mix of physics, astrology and philosophy); and the superhero, the son of a human father and an alien mother, grew up not on Krypton but in a monastery in Ladakh, gaining all manner of superpowers simply through his expertise in yoga!

For someone who had grown up idolizing *Star Trek*, to be cast as the hero of an indigenous series in the same genre was beyond exciting—my head was full of so many ideas for the series that I wanted to write and direct it myself! I didn't, of course—Ketan was a very capable director indeed—but I did talk about my ideas with him extensively. I urged him to think about *Vyom*—at least in terms of the messaging— as a series for adults, like *Star Trek* was, and not just as Sunday-morning entertainment for kids. Children would watch a sci-fi series with a superhero anyway, but it would become a truly great series only when it also appealed to adults. Unfortunately for me, Ketan was not open to my ideas. When he fell ill in the middle of filming, a new director, who was far more receptive, took over, but by then, it was too late to change much. So *Vyom* was shot as it had originally been planned, and a huge opportunity, at least in my opinion, was lost. I thought the series was horrendous.

As usually happened when I did not like something, *Vyom* went on to become a huge hit and enjoyed a cult following in India. Kids—and adults!—loved the overstuffed plot that had clichés drawn as much from *Chandamama* as from every cheesy international story in the genre—time machines, interdimensional travel, a Queen of Sheba checklist of four esoteric enemy-destroying objects (a compass, a herb, a weapon, a fuel) to be collected from across the solar system, a crystal with the ability to weaken the otherwise impenetrable shield of the ruler of the Parajeevs (a race of aliens), an orphan hero who is desperately seeking his origins—Were my parents humans or Parajeevs? Were they heroes or villains?—and, of course, a beautiful alien woman with a heart of gold.

Vyom's magic has lasted to this day. In airports, at running meets, in the meeting rooms of companies that have offered to sponsor an event I am hosting, at giant forums to which I have been invited as a speaker, people from across the board—CISF jawans, CEOs, customs officers, additional commissioners of police, bank managers, heads of marketing—will come to me and tell me, with stars in their eyes, how much they enjoyed watching the adventures of Captain Vyom. To them, despite the many years that have passed since *Vyom* was aired, despite the fact that, with my grey hair and boring shorts and bare feet, I look nothing like that spiffy superhero of their childhood fantasies, despite the fact that I have played so many other roles on-screen these past twenty years—I will never just be the actor who played Captain Vyom. To them, I am, simply, Captain Vyom himself. I don't know about you, but I believe that that kind of adulation is a touch difficult for a wooden actor to come by.

~

It was around the time that I was shooting for *A Mouthful of Sky* that I began to smoke. It wasn't as if I had never tried it before—when I was only twelve, on the urging of the boy who lived next door, I had picked up cigarette stubs from the street and made a habit of smoking them—but it was only around 1995 that I began to smoke, well, *properly*.

I was thirty by this time, which is hardly the age at which anyone starts smoking. I had stayed off the cigarettes throughout my modelling years, partly because I had still had the sportsman's hangover and partly because I was bingeing so much on alcohol. Also, ramp shows and photo shoots (I did far more of the former than the latter) were occasional affairs and rarely took more than half a day to wrap up. In other words, there was no time to get bored enough, or stressed enough, to pick up a fag.

Things were very different in the television studios, however. I was working very hard on *Vyom*, which meant long hours on the sets, for months on end, hanging out with the same set of people. I found the 'being indoors' bit pretty stressful—I liked to be out and about, moving, doing things in the open air. Plus, to an introvert like me, hanging out with people for such a big part of the day was a different, but equally debilitating, kind of stress. One way to counter the claustrophobia and cabin fever was to try what everyone else around me swore were the two best ways to bust every kind of stress—drinking chai, which was free and came around every hour, and/or lighting up a fag, which, at only Rs 1.50 a pop, was eminently affordable to everyone. And that's how I picked up two terrible habits, neither of which I had indulged in before.

Given my obsessive streak, it was only natural that once I began to smoke, I would do it like it was going out of fashion. For years, from about 1998 and all the way until 2004, when I ran my first half-marathon, I went through some thirty cigarettes a day. Bollywood, where I made my debut with the crime-thriller *Tarkieb* in the year 2000, helped the habit along—hanging around on a Bollywood set was far more stressful, I discovered, than hanging around in a television studio, because all you did on a film set was wait! You waited for the make-up guy to show up, you waited for the spot boys to set up, you waited for the other actors to arrive (or not!), you waited for everyone else to give their takes, you waited and waited and waited, and then you gave your three-minute shot for the day. Then you came back the next day and did it all over again. It was mind-numbingly boring, and the only real way to pass the time was to smoke. That isn't really a defensible excuse, though—to date, smoking remains the stupidest thing I have ever done.

One thing that saved me from getting irrevocably addicted to smoking was that it was absolutely forbidden at home. My dad had been a hard smoker for many years, and Aai disapproved of cigarettes wholeheartedly. The other was that, because of some subconscious guilt about smoking, I had never actually bought myself a cigarette through my smoking years; I had only ever bummed them off others. Somehow, that had felt like less of a sin.

By 2001, however, the self-deception was wearing thin—I realized that my smoking was turning into something truly dangerous, and had to stop. Even with that realization, it took me three whole years to wean myself off cigarettes; in sharp contrast, my strong-willed dad, when he had decided to stop, had been able to do it in twenty-four hours. What finally pushed me over the edge was the discovery, when I began training for the inaugural Mumbai marathon in 2003, that I was seriously out of shape and that a lot of it could be attributed to my smoking habit. That was exactly the kick in the pants a sportsman needed. By 2004, I was only smoking very occasionally; soon after, I stopped entirely.

I am often asked how a thirty-ciggies-a-day guy could become so completely clean. What was my regimen? Did I use a nicotine patch? How bad were the withdrawal symptoms? Well, I don't know whether it will work for you, but the method I used to cure myself of that particular madness was procrastination. Yeah, that thing that most of us are naturally so good at. Let me explain how it works. If you are a smoker, you know that the longing for a drag is not a constant one; it assails you in waves. Here's my advice— when the urge comes upon you, procrastinate. Tell yourself you will get a cigarette in ten minutes, and continue doing what you're doing. If you consciously let ten minutes pass, you will notice that the urge has subsided; you will not feel as strongly about needing a cigarette any more. Sooner rather than later, you will not need a cigarette at all!

That may sound disingenuous, or at best, simplistic. But quitting smoking isn't about nicotine patches; it's really a choice that you make. When you make that choice unequivocally, giving yourself no quarter, leaving yourself no escape routes at all, whatever method you use will work; it becomes easy to quit. And that's the honest truth.

In 2017, I got to be part of *I Can, You Can*, a very cool adventure reality show launched by video-on-demand service Viu, in partnership with Nicotex, a company that makes nicotine patches to help smokers quit. The idea was that since quitting smoking was supposedly as difficult as climbing Everest, Nicotex would sponsor three smokers, each of them tagged with a quitter (ex-smoker), to actually trek to Everest base camp. Encouraged by his quitter, inspired by the joys of a healthy lifestyle and, possibly, even unnerved by how bad his own lung capacity was compared to his teammate's, each smoker would (hopefully) end up kicking the habit on the way to the top, thus conquering his own personal Everest. The entire journey was produced by BBC Worldwide India as a six-part series and telecast on Viu and National Geographic Channel.

As a celebrity quitter and athlete, I got to lead the group of six to Everest base camp. For me, personally, apart from the fabulous trek itself, *I Can, You Can* was a great opportunity to share my own quitting story and my journey beyond smoking, not just with the six people in the group but with thousands of smokers across the country—each episode has been viewed hundreds of thousands of times on YouTube—hopefully inspiring them to follow in the same path. As a complete bonus, I got to take the first step of a dream journey that has been part of every bucket list I've made since I was a boy—summiting Everest!

And they say quitters never prosper. Ha!

~

You know the stories of how I missed my chance of a Bollywood debut in a Mansoor Khan film, and my chance to debut as a transvestite. But Bollywood and I were not done with missed opportunities yet. The third time around, I lost out on a lead role in a Ram Gopal Varma (RGV) film.

It was while I was shooting *Sea Hawks* that I was approached by RGV, who wanted to cast me in his obsessive-lover flick, *Pyar Tune Kya Kiya*. But finding dates for a movie shoot in an already packed TV-shoot schedule was difficult. Plus, to my mind, juggling two commitments was unfair to both directors. The plot didn't get me going either, so I declined without a second thought. RGV was considered a real hotshot at the time—an award-winning director from south India who had made a great impression with his Bollywood debut, *Shool*—and he didn't take the rejection well. When I told Shivam Nair, the director of *Sea Hawks*, that I had refused RGV's offer because I didn't think it would be fair to him, he was aghast. RGV had been his mentor and Shivam idolized him. He sent me back to RGV, post-haste, to let him know I had changed my mind. But when I met him, just two days after I had declined his offer, RGV would hear nothing of what I had to say. 'I have cast Manoj Bajpayee,' he told me shortly. 'The role does not exist any more.' Ouch.

As it turned out, Manoj Bajpayee did not end up playing the lead. The film was delayed for almost a year, and when it finally went into production, it had Fardeen Khan as the hero. That meant only one thing—RGV could have put me back into the film when Manoj dropped out, but he had *chosen* not to. Oh well.

Pyar Tune Kya Kiya was a huge 2001 hit and garnered a lot of accolades for Urmila Matondkar, who played the obsessed lover. A year or so later, when RGV wandered on to the sets of a film that my company, E-Motion, was producing, I went over to ask him if he was still mad at me. He was all smiles, all charm. 'Of course not,' he said. 'Who told you I was ever mad at you?' Umm . . . lots of people, RGV.

And thus it was that I finally made my Bollywood debut in *Tarkieb*, a crime drama that released in 2000, starring Nana Patekar as the investigating detective and Tabu as the murder victim. The murder takes place in an army cantonment, and four of the (promiscuous) victim's lovers are the prime suspects. I played one of the suspects, Captain Ajit Verma. The film didn't make much of a mark at the box office.

The next significant movie to come my way was the 2002 spy thriller *16 December*, in which I played an officer from the Internal Revenue Service. It was directed by a first-time director, but it was an unusual story with a taut plot and was received very well. But it was the other film that released in 2002 that brought me official recognition as an actor of some note—for my role as the large-hearted, dutiful, innocent Aravasu in *Agnivarsha*, a film adaptation of Girish Karnad's play *The Fire and the Rain*, based on a story from the Mahabharata, I was nominated for the Star Screen Awards in the Best Supporting Actor category. To me, though, the highlight of being part of *Agnivarsha* was that I got to share screen time with Amitabh Bachchan himself. Yes sirree, Mr Bachchan played the king of the Devas, Indra, in the film!

But I had no time to dwell on this, for I was now deep in the throes of a new and most exciting project with my own film- and television-production company. For the past six years, E-Motion had been busy—apart from *Margarita*, which was written by Vinay Pathak and featured Rajeshwari Sachdev as the female lead, we had produced serials like *Hubahu* and *Hip Hip Hurray!* and a bunch of non-fiction television content for various channels. In 2002, we were finally ready to take our game to the next level and produce our own feature film—*Rules: Pyaar ka Superhit Formula*. My business partner, Parvati, was going to direct it, and I was going to star in it.

Rules, which released in 2003, was a breezy, light-hearted, feel-good romantic comedy. It featured Meera Vasudevan as Radha, a photographer's assistant, who is madly in love with supermodel Vikram Verma (played by yours truly). Unfortunately, Vikram only ever has eyes for his pouty girlfriend, Maggie. So Radha sighs and mopes, until her feisty grandmother, played by the incredible veteran actress Tanuja, notices her distress and asks her what the matter is. When Radha reveals that it is an affair of the heart, her grandmother gives her what she insists is a fail-safe formula, involving five rules, to win her lover boy. Simply follow these rules, says Grandma, and he will fall for you, hook, line and sinker. Initially sceptical, Radha does as her grandma says and is stunned when, a few weeks later, Vikram declares his love for her. But now Radha is in a quandary—she isn't sure whether she herself *really* loves him, and feels guilty about having 'trapped' him using a formula. And so on and so forth.

All of us at E-Motion, and the entire crew of *Rules*, were thrilled when the film was well received, both by the movie-going public and by critics. Everyone who saw it, including those who did not give it a five-star rating, described it as different, fresh and sweet. This last adjective—sweet—seemed, to viewers, to capture the most fundamental vibe of *Rules*, and that made me preen more than a little. Because, ladies and gentlemen, it was I—ahem!—who came up with a structure for the film and a lot of the story, including the five rules that make up the love formula. And what were those rules?

- Rule no. 1—If you want him to notice you, ignore him.
- Rule no. 2—Allow him ample space to come after you.
- Rule no. 3—Be unpredictable; never let him feel that he has understood you completely.
- Rule no. 4—Don't let him see, ever, that he has the ability to hurt you emotionally.

- Rule no. 5—Praise him constantly, so that he feels secure enough to say 'I love you'.

People were sceptical about man-about-town Milind—he of the long trail of girlfriends—scripting the rules for love. After all, they scoffed, what can someone who can get any woman he wants know about love? But my close friends, who had always looked to me for relationship advice, swore they did not know who could have done it better.

I tend to agree with my friends. After all, who else but someone who has been in very many different relationships— all of them loving, most of them long-term, each one a committed relationship while it lasted—would know how to snag someone? More importantly, who but someone who has been at the receiving end of so many advances would know what works to pique a man's interest and what does exactly the opposite?

Plus, I just happen to be very, very good at reading people. I don't know if the skill was something I was born with or is something I have developed over the years, but I can tell, very soon after meeting someone, what makes him or her tick. I have always found it very easy to 'manipulate'—such a terrible word, evoking all kinds of negative emotions, but I mean it only in a very literal sense here—people to do what I want them to do. At its most basic, this ability translates into knowing exactly what to say and do to make someone fall in love with me, or, at the very least, imagine they have fallen in love with me. Most people are very transparent, very naive.

It is precisely because I have this ability that I have always been militant about never using it on my girlfriends, my wife, or the people closest and dearest to me. As Radha realizes in *Rules*, there is no joy in having someone fall in love with you when you know you have manipulated them to make it happen. In your closest relationships at least, you want to believe that people love you and care for you simply for who you are.

But my tendency to be manipulative—of people and situations—is a useful ability to have in the workplace. As I have gotten older, I have learnt to use it to simplify my life. I never do anything but what I really want to do any more. For everything else that I want to explore—whether because it has the potential to make me money or because it is a worthy cause or simply something that piques my interest—I just put the word out and wait for someone who is either already doing it or has a passion for it to find me. When she does, I either agree to be the brand ambassador for, and/or a stakeholder in, her existing business, or urge her to start a business that I will invest in. Most people realize that celebrities have the ability to attract both money and visibility for a brand and are happy to collaborate.

That's it! With that, I become the director of a trust or charity that I believe in, or part owner of a business that I am proud to be associated with! (This last is very important to me—in all my years as a model or an actor, I have never endorsed a product that could cause harm or that I did not personally believe in, which meant alcohol, cigarettes, sodas and junk food were automatically out.) Now all I have to do is support my business partner while she goes after her dreams, focusing her energies on what she is good at and loves best.

Yes, *she*. I don't know if you have noticed it yet, but my partners in business have most often been, and continue to be, women.

After my first business venture as part-owner of an event management agency with my then girlfriend, I partnered with Parvati for E-Motion Pictures, which became Face Entertainment (its current avatar) when two more partners—both women—came on board. In 2003, I went into partnership with my designer friend Madhu Jain—she is celebrated, then and now, as one of the country's best-known craft revivalists and textile conservationists—to set up Projekt-M, a design initiative through which we hoped to showcase and popularize a variety of sustainable fabrics and traditional weaving and embroidery styles. One of our more memorable outings came in 2004, when Projekt-M travelled to Delhi to show a collection of bamboo-based clothing at the VII World Bamboo Congress—Madhu and I had designed a grand spectacle, which included 20-feet-high puppets telling the folk story of how bamboo came to earth.

In 2008, with entrepreneur Reema Sanghavi, I started an event-management company called Maximus. Today, one of our most popular and best-known properties, which we promote in collaboration with our NGO, United Sisters Foundation, is Pinkathon, India's biggest women's run.

In 2014, after sampling, at the Pune Marathon Expo, a particularly yummy—and filling—cereal bar, which I was assured was also healthy, I entered into partnership with Shilpa Phadke, the creative force behind On the Run, the company that had produced those bars. The bars, each a mini meal, now retail in over 400 stores across the country. It makes me feel very chuffed that one of my companies makes a wonderful additive- and preservative-free snack for runners, even though I have done very little actual work for the company since I joined, except perhaps chomping my way through a mountain of On the Run bars.

In 2016, entrepreneurs Raga D'Silva and Nicola Fenton, partners in a UK-based talent-management company called Red Hot Mirchi Global, met Reema at an event they all happened to be attending. When they mentioned to Reema what they did—manage motivational speakers— her antennae went up. I had been talking for years about setting up a similar company in India, and this seemed the perfect fit. The four of us got together, explored going into partnership, agreed that it sounded like a good idea and shook hands on the deal. And just like that, Reema and I became part-owners of a new talent-management company called Speaking Minds, which today brings to India some of the most inspiring motivational speakers from all over the world. More recently, I have become associated with the Bangalore-based Active Holiday Company (AHC), founded by travel entrepreneur Gauri Jayaram, which specializes in marathon tourism—it organizes trips for groups of Indian runners to the world's premier marathons and takes care of all details, right from getting them an entry into the race. In every sense, it is a company I definitely wanted a piece of.

See? *She!*

I'm not sure if I am more comfortable working with women because I grew up around four of them or because I find them naturally—and consistently—more empathetic, hard-working, committed, creative and loyal, but that has been the truth of my life. The sardar who told Aai on the way to the Bhakra–Nangal Dam that I would always be surrounded by women certainly knew what he was talking about!

KILOMETRE 37.8—GIRGAUM CHOWPATTY

6TH STANDARD CHARTERED MUMBAI MARATHON, SUNDAY, 18 JANUARY 2009

For the first couple of kilometres or so after my quadriceps gave up, I kept going without really realizing it. My body had locked itself into a rhythm for the past three hours, and it kept going, putting one foot in front of the other like a bad habit it could not break. My mind, on the other hand, was spacing out, drifting in and out of lucid thought as the millions of pain receptors in my legs slammed it with a relentless tirade of agony, hammering their message home in ways that could not be ignored.

By the time I had passed Haji Ali, however, there was nothing unconscious or automaton-like about my steps. Each step was an effort that I was making, with the full knowledge that I was making it. In my lucid moments, just to keep my mind alert for longer and send myself whatever positive vibes I could, I carried on a conversation in my head with an imaginary listener about the miracle of the human body, and what an advanced, evolved machine it was.

Do you know, I asked my listener, that a human being never really drops from exhaustion? His legs, his upright spine, have evolved for persistence hunting, for foraging for food, to help him maintain superiority over so many other animals, many of them far bigger, stronger and more fearsome than himself, for no less than 10,000 years! How do you think this creature, the human, is able to outrun these much-faster creatures on his puny legs with the puny muscles? Because, my friend, running on four legs is inefficient—it compromises lung capacity. An animal, even the fastest there is, cannot keep up that extreme speed for more than a few seconds at a time. It can't even run at half those speeds for a very long period. And when it drops, when it can't go on any more, there is always a human coming up the path, or, more often, a pack of them, a pack that has been patiently jogging behind the animal for over an hour, and is still in excellent shape. When the animal sees them, it knows its time has come.

I was zoning out again as fresh shafts of pain dug their talons into my legs. The gentle rise of Cumballa Hill had turned into a veritable Himalayan ascent on my way back, and there were still 7 kilometres to go. For once in my life, it was more comfortable to dwell on the past than look ahead, so I did.

Almost 36 kilometres done, I exulted, a mere 7 to go. Take joy in the pain, it won't last much longer!

My imaginary friend shook his head at that. I always knew that about you, he said sadly, but now it's confirmed. You are a freak. Aha, I said, and you think that freaks are a minority, don't you? That's where you're wrong, my friend. Freaks are the majority. We are all capable of so much more than we believe we are—we choose not to explore our inner freak simply because we are terrified to go there, to lock eyes with our potential. Because once we have, you see, there is no excuse for not fulfilling it.

We are called an intelligent species, and we are. As a collective, we are inordinately powerful. As individuals against the environment, we have not only survived but thrived, for over ten millennia. I'll tell you where we've sort of lost the plot, though—in all the thousands of years we've spent making things better for ourselves outside of us, we have disconnected from what is inside. We have figured out how to listen to signals from across the universe but lost the ability to read the signals our bodies are sending us. We have swapped our running muscles for jobs that grow only the gluteus maximus and make us ill and slow. We have outsourced our bodies, our memories, our thoughts and our brains to the religion and the crutch called technology, and then we wonder stupidly why we are losing our minds.

We have been gifted so many faculties—but you either use 'em or lose 'em, my friend, it's that simple. Every creature, every race of creatures, adapts to a higher order or a lower order—

that's the basis of evolutionary biology. We are the only race that can make a conscious choice about which way we want to go, and it's ridiculous how often we make the unintelligent one. Every time you reach higher, you improve the quality of your life; each time you skip your daily fitness schedule or reach for a drink too many, you degrade it—you can see this happen in a single lifetime, to people around you, to yourself. Each time you make a choice to be stressed about something—and it's a choice, no debate about that!—you weaken your immune system. You invite disease in, and allow it to take over—your stressed-out mind does not allow your body to stay strong. The more we make wrong choices as a collective, the more we destroy ourselves as a species. Believe me, it isn't a natural calamity that will wipe us off the face of the earth, it is the daily self-degradation that we actively—and consciously—participate in that will be our undoing.

That's why I run, my friend. I run so that I do not lose my connections to my ancestors, my body, my environment, the earth, my humanness. I run to feel alive, to stay alive.

Nice speech, applauded my listener. Except you are about to die.

He was right. While I had been nattering on, almost delirious, he had been keeping a close eye on my physical condition and knew it was all but over. I had just hobbled out on to Marine Drive at Girgaum Chowpatty, but this time around, the vast sweep of Back Bay and the expanse of the

Arabian Sea, shimmering fiercely in the sun, brought me no joy. I didn't even see it. Unable to go on, whether by will or habit, my entire body racked with pain, I crumpled against the barriers lining the route, slid to the ground and blacked out.

5

STARRY-EYED

'If I had followed my better judgement always, my life
would have been a very dull one.'

—Edgar Rice Burroughs

But let's go back now to the movies. And let's talk about the
film where I met my first wife.

Around 2004, I was approached by a young Indian
film-maker who had become a name to watch out for after
his debut film *Samsara*, released in 2001, had struck gold,
sweeping some thirty international awards. He had a very
unusual name—Pan Nalin (he told me later that his given
name was Nalin Kumar Pandya, and that he had grown up
in various cities of Gujarat, graduating from the National
Institute of Design at Ahmedabad before coming to Bombay
to make films)—and he was getting ready to shoot his second

film. Would I consider, he asked me, playing the male lead in his new film?

I read up everything I found about Nalin (you may be more familiar with him as the director of the 2015 Bollywood film *Angry Indian Goddesses*). I watched *Samsara*, a story about the conflict between spirituality and the sexual urge—a young Buddhist monk called Tashi comes out of a cave after three years of intense meditation, only to promptly and uncontrollably fall in love with a woman— and was fascinated by Nalin's take on human frailty and the kind of punishing discipline any quest demands. His next film, for which he had me in mind, was also an intense love story, based on the mystical Indian and Buddhist themes of karma and rebirth and immortality. It spanned two centuries, running from the nineteenth to the twenty-first, and it played out in locations as diverse as the ancient Silk Road and the modern metropolis of Tokyo. It was also, as *Samsara* had been, an international collaboration, a French– German–Indian independent film that was tentatively titled *La Vallée des Fleurs—Valley of Flowers*.

Thinking about it, I realized there was really no way I could lose with this one—the director's perspective was fresh, the premise promising and the location breathtaking (quite literally, too, as I was to discover—there was no way I could smoke in the rarefied, oxygen-deficient air of Ladakh; for someone trying to quit, it was exactly what the doctor had ordered). Plus, I would be riding horses a lot—the hero of the film was a bandit who made his living by robbing caravans travelling along the Silk Road in the higher Himalayas—and that sounded like fun. My only reservation with the film was that it was going to be a Hindi film. I wished they had chosen to make it a Ladakhi film instead; it would have been truer to the story and the landscape. But that was a mere creative quibble—overall, *Valley* would be vastly different from anything I had ever done before, and what could be more exciting for an experience-junkie like me who loved the outdoors? I accepted Nalin's offer without further ado.

Let me give you a little summary of the plot before we go on. *Valley of Flowers* is the story of star-crossed lovers Jalan and Ushna. Jalan rides at the head of a gang of bandits who have walked away from the constraining rules of civil society and live wild and free in the mountains. One day, a beautiful woman emerges from nowhere, introduces herself as Ushna, and, claiming that she remembers Jalan from a previous life, asks to be allowed to ride with him. Jalan's men are completely opposed to the idea of having a stranger, and that too a woman, join their all-male crew, but Jalan, enraptured by Ushna's other-worldly beauty and mystical aura, cannot refuse her.

Luckily for Jalan, Ushna proves to be an asset to the gang. She knows the terrain much better than Jalan and his men, besides being an excellent rider and strategist.

Inevitably, Jalan and Ushna fall madly in love, and Jalan, slowly but surely, becomes alienated from his men. After an astrologer tells the lovers that it is not in their fates to be united, Ushna directs Jalan to steal people's energies instead of their possessions, and teaches him how to do it. Once they gather enough, she tells him, the two of them will be powerful enough to change their destinies. This, of course, goes against the natural laws of the universe, and is bound to bring retribution down on their heads, but so besotted are the two that they continue along this dangerous path. Fearing that something is not quite right with Ushna, Jalan's men split with him and go their own way.

Whispers of the strange happenings along the Silk Road reach the ears of the demon hunter Yeti (played by Naseeruddin Shah—yes, he was in the film as well!), who recognizes Ushna from the travellers' description as an immortal who has no business meddling with the world of mortals. He sets off on her trail, determined to capture her and send her back to where she belongs. The chase begins, but the two lovers elude him and end up at a monastery where it is rumoured that a monk has discovered the formula to the elixir of immortality. Against their better judgement— Ushna wonders, momentarily, if it might not be better for the two to live out the natural spans of their lives in the Valley of Flowers—the lovers drink the elixir, not realizing that while it does have the power to turn a mortal (Jalan) into an immortal, it also reverses immortality, turning an immortal (Ushna) into a mortal. When Yeti catches up with them the next day, Jalan, boasting to him that he (Yeti) has no power over them now, asks Ushna to shoot him while he does the same to her. They shoot each other, but while Jalan is unharmed, Ushna falls to the floor in a heap, quite dead.

Distraught, Jalan roams the world for the next two centuries, searching in vain for his beloved Ushna. The twenty-first century finds him in Tokyo, in his new identity as the Indian doctor Jalan Otsai, a legalized practitioner of euthanasia. Hated and feared by the locals, who believe nature should be allowed to take its own course, Jalan is frequently in the news. One day, he is spotted on television by a singer called Sayuri, who is really Ushna serving out her karma in her fifth human reincarnation. Ecstatic, Sayuri rushes to be reunited with Jalan, who gives her the last remaining drops of the elixir he has carried on his person for 200 years. Yeti, who has been keeping a beady eye on the two, warns them that meddling with the fates never ends well, but the couple is rejoicing too much to pay him heed.

I'm not giving away the twist in the tale here. That would be unfair to the movie's writers, among whom was—hold your breath—Anurag Kashyap himself, in his pre–*Black Friday* days. Suffice it to say that *Valley of Flowers*—an epic tale at 2 hours 35 minutes—was received very well when it released in 2006 and still boasts a decent 7.0 rating on IMDb. It also won Nalin the Jury Award at the 2007 Indian Film Festival of Los Angeles for Best Feature Film, and received four nominations the same year at the Indo-American Arts Council Awards, including for Best Picture and Best Director.

Of course, all this was still to come. My own story with *Valley of Flowers* began in 2004, on location in Ladakh, when I met the young French actress Mylène Jampanoï. Her unusual looks came from her dad, who was Chinese, and her mum, who was French–Breton. I disliked her on sight. Neither of us had any idea who the other was, but by the end of the first couple of days of shooting, we had made our impressions of each other—I thought she was a terrible actor and blamed the casting crew for picking her, and she—surprise, surprise!—thought exactly the same of me. She had also realized, from the reactions of the locals, that I was something of a big noise in these parts, and that probably made her feel a little insecure.

One evening, very soon after the first shooting schedule had begun, she walked up to me after pack-up. 'Listen,' she said (rather snottily, I thought), 'I believe you are a well-known model and Bollywood (she said the word like it was an insult) actor. Please don't spoil the movie.' And she turned on her heel and walked away, leaving me feeling most indignant. It was exactly the kind of opening that signalled the beginning of every Bollywood-style romance, although I didn't see it that way until much later. At that time, I was only hugely annoyed at the thought of being stuck with her for the next three months.

I'm not sure how much of the fact that we were passionate on-screen lovers helped our own romance along, but one month before the Ladakh schedule wrapped up, we had professed our real-life love for each other. Everything seemed to be against us—I was thirty-nine then, she eighteen years younger; it was going to be a long-distance relationship for the foreseeable future; and although there was the Japan schedule of the movie left to shoot, she wasn't going to be in it, so this was really the end of our official time together. But none of that seemed to matter a whit, to either of us, in the heady rush of love.

When *Valley of Flowers* moved to Japan for its second shooting schedule, Mylène made a trip there to be with me. For the next two years, we spoke to each other often and met when we could, both of us equally determined to make it work. On my part, whenever I found the time, I made trips to Paris to see her.

But it was hard. She was a struggling young model and actress, trying to find a foothold in the small, fussy French film industry, and she was often broke. She was also trying to get acting assignments in Hollywood, but there were very few opportunities available for someone of her ethnicity then (not to say that much has changed today). The fact that she came from the south of France made her a complete outsider even in Paris, so Hollywood was a very distant dream.

Despite all this, both of us stayed seriously committed to the relationship. When Mylène came to India in 2006 to do the promo tours for the film, I whisked her away to Goa, where my mother's roots are, and got married to her in a small, intimate ceremony in an old Portuguese house—with a very happy Aai (my mum loved Mylène, as she had all my other girlfriends), my sisters and a few friends in attendance. The ceremony was somewhat marred by the fact that I had just been diagnosed with jaundice—what are the odds that as dire a thing as jaundice should descend on someone who is so seldom ill, on the eve of his wedding day?—but neither of us let that dampen our spirits.

For the next two years, we soldiered on, tossing around all kinds of alternative scenarios to the awful one that was our reality, and which, as we both were rapidly realizing, was untenable. Sadly, the only scenario that could work, which involved one of us moving for at least a few years to the other's country, always played out as the irresistible force meeting the immovable object; neither of us was willing to even consider it. Naturally, I thought it made a lot more sense for her to move to India—I was already an established name here, I had work and income coming my way that could comfortably support the two of us—but Mylène was fiercely independent and she, understandably, didn't see it quite the way I did.

I often ask myself why I was so eager to seal the deal with Mylène via the ultimate commitment, marriage, when I had done quite well in other, equally meaningful, long-term relationships, some of which had lasted way longer than this one and been far less impractical. I don't really have an answer to that one, except to say that it had seemed right at that time, for the both of us. Perhaps it was precisely because I realized how pie in the sky this moving-countries scenario was that I sought to make it more permanent, at least on paper; perhaps I hoped that this ultimate demonstration of commitment on both our parts would nudge the universe to drop a miracle into our laps.

But the universe wasn't biting. By 2008, it was clear that a beautiful forever for our own star-crossed love story was just as impossible and unattainable as it had been for Jalan and Ushna. With a lot of sadness but no regret—for we were both convinced by then that what we were doing was best for both of us—Mylène and I went our separate ways in 2009.

~

'I'm a bad man. I'm the prettiest thing that ever lived.'

—Muhammad Ali

Through the tumultuous years of my courtship and marriage to Mylène and beyond, my movie career continued sporadic but unabated. And although I have never yet played a lead role and have remained an outsider in Bollywood—for the industry sees me as too 'westernized'—I have enjoyed playing supporting roles in some very good movies—*Bheja Fry*, *Bajirao Mastani* (in which I played Ambaji Pant, Bajirao's shaven-headed mentor) and, most recently, *Chef* (in which I played Biju, the rich guy courting the ex-wife of the eponymous chef played by Saif Ali Khan).

Between 2007 and 2013, I was cast in four Tamil films—*Pachaikili Muthucharam* (a copy of *Derailed*, directed by Gautam Menon), the top-grossing Karthi hit *Paiyaa*, the action comedy *Alex Pandian* (also starring Karthi) and the box office bomb *Vithagan*. All of them netted me decent reviews for my portrayal of goons, named Lawrence, Baali, Alvin Martin and Badri respectively. I was also in a spectacularly bad Telugu film called *Satyameva Jayathe* in 2009. In the end, I stopped accepting roles in south Indian cinema—it can get a little tedious to play a baddie—and the same kind of straight-up baddie, without texture or nuance—all the time, especially in a language you don't know.

It's a rum thing, but for all the press I get about how 'hot' and 'sexy' I am—no interview with a female journalist, no encounter with a female fan, has ever begun without her first saying something complimentary about my looks, followed almost always by (pick one), 'My mom is also a fan/ my twenty-year-old daughter is also a fan/my *grandmother* is a fan' (not even kidding!)—I have never been cast as the romantic lead in any Indian film to date (apart from *Rules*, in which I decided to cast myself as one)! It could be that actors get typecast because directors have no imagination, but it could also be something entirely else that I'm completely missing. I'd love to know if you have any theories on why south Indian directors, particularly, only saw me as the perfect villain—it would be good to put that ghost to rest.

The year 2009 was also when I snagged my first Marathi film, *Gandha* (*Smell*), which had a very interesting structure, featuring three different stories, each with smell as the leitmotif. *Gandha* went on to win its writer, Sachin Kundalkar, the National Award for Best Screenplay. I have also been a part of two other award-winning Marathi films—*Samhita*, which used the narrative of a story within a story very cleverly, and the 2015 political thriller *Nagrik*. My 'Et tu, Brute' moment with Marathi cinema happened when I won a Maharashtra State Film Award, my only one so far, for *Nagrik*—in the category of Best Actor in a, erm, *Negative* Role.

Right. Moving on.

Oh, wait. Just to tie all this up nicely, I must mention the two extravagant Swedish period productions I was part of (they were predominantly Swedish, but had Danish, Finnish, Norwegian and German involvement as well). The two films—*Arn: Tempelriddaren* (*Arn: The Knight Templar*) and its sequel, *Arn: Riket vid vägens slut* (Arn: The Kingdom at Road's End)—were released in Sweden in 2007 and 2008, and still hold the record for the most expensive productions in Swedish cinema ever.

The films tell the story of Arn Magnusson, son of the powerful chieftain of Sweden's Folkung dynasty in the twelfth century, against the background of the Crusades. Arn grows up in a monastery but is trained to be a warrior by one of the monks, a former member of the Knights Templar, who believes he is not meant to be a monk but a soldier of Christ. One day, while wandering in the woods, Arn kills two men who are harassing a girl into marriage. Even though his action had been purely an act of self-defence, performed in the process of saving a woman's honour, the monks tell him he cannot live in the monastery any more and send him back to his family. Once there, Arn gets completely embroiled in the fractious war that his family is fighting with other prominent Swedish families for the crown of Västra Götaland.

As might be expected, plenty of political intrigue is afoot, and Arn, who is becoming too dangerous to the other players, is excommunicated along with his fiancée, for indulging in sexual relations before marriage. Both are forced to undertake twenty years of solitary penance to expunge their sin—Cecilia in a convent and Arn as a member of the Knights Templar in the Holy Land, fighting against the enemies of Christianity.

Arn discharges his duties as a Templar honourably for many years. One day, while pursuing a band of thieves, he saves the life of a stranger being attacked by the gang, and realizes too late that the person he has rescued is the worst enemy of all Christendom, Sultan Saladin himself. A grateful Saladin warns Arn to stay away from Jerusalem, against which his Muslim forces are about to launch a most vicious Holy War. But brave Arn, leading a small and straggly band of Christian soldiers, scuppers Saladin's plans by cutting his mighty army off at the pass. Saladin flees to Cairo, and Jerusalem is saved—at least for the time being. Arn is released from service and is finally free to go back to his beloved Cecilia.

I played Saladin in the movie and enjoyed myself thoroughly. It's always a great experience to be part of an international production—I love the exposure it gives me, on so many levels, to a different culture.

I can see you chuckling to yourself. They cast him as the bad guy *again*, you're thinking. But Saladin wasn't the *bad* guy, you know. He was the hero of the Crusades as far as the Arabs were concerned, defending their own Holy Land against the 'barbaric' Christians. And, FYI, he did get Jerusalem eventually. Ha, you say, that may be so when you take the long view of history. In the movie, though, there was only one hero, only one good guy, and his name was Arn.

Oh, all right. I admit it. It didn't really matter whether the casting director was south Indian or Marathi, or Swedish—they always saw me as the bad guy. I must remember to tell Aai of this epiphany I've had—she'll have a hearty laugh at my expense, and say, 'What have I always told you? You *don't* look like a hero.' Ah well, mum's always been the (last) word.

KILOMETRE 42.5—CHHATRAPATI SHIVAJI TERMINUS

6TH STANDARD CHARTERED MUMBAI MARATHON, SUNDAY, 18 JANUARY 2009

'Get up! Come on! You've got to finish this! There isn't a long way to go!'

I was floating in and out of consciousness. A female voice was yelling something incoherent into my ears, shaking me. I wished she wouldn't—I just wanted to stay where I was. Who cared about finishing the race when the beguiling alternative of surrendering to the exhaustion was right in front of me?

But the woman (women?) wouldn't stop speaking. Small, strong hands began to rub my legs vigorously, and a pungent, somehow-familiar scent assailed my nostrils. Ah yes! In another lifetime, I had known that distinctive smell—pain sprays, muscle relaxant gels, balms, they all smelt like that. Poor thing,

I thought to myself, she really wants me to get up and run—how do I tell her that she's wasting her time?

'Come on! You can do this!'

I was zoning out again. I found myself back at the Mahatma Gandhi Memorial Swimming Pool, a boy of ten, stroking furiously away towards the finish, hearing, every time I surfaced, my coach's voice urging me along: 'Come on! Keep swimming! You can do this!' But his voice sounded high-pitched, like a woman's. Was it Aai, then, who was cheering me on? I'd find out later. For now, I just needed to keep swimming.

So I did, but suddenly day had turned into night, and I found myself in the open sea, swimming as hard as I could, conscious of some lurking danger and frantic to get away from it. But I couldn't; before I knew it, I had got tangled up in a fishing net and was thrashing about hopelessly, unable to break water, knowing with chilling certainty that I was going to die.

And I might have, if another swimmer hadn't appeared out of nowhere beside me. I recognized him instantly—he was my long-time friend and ace swimmer, Vinod Ghadge. We couldn't speak underwater, but his hands were working furiously, untangling me from the net. Moments later, he gave me a thumbs up—I was good to go. When I looked again, he had disappeared. But my mind was suddenly crystal clear.

'Get up! Come on! You've got to do this! I will be with you all the way!'

I stood up. I had completely forgotten that I had dedicated my debut marathon to Vinod. Now that he had come by to remind me himself, there was no way I was not going to finish, whether it took five hours or fifty.

I began to hobble down Marine Drive, my cheerleader and calf-masseuse by my side. I must have looked at her at some point, but her face never registered, only her voice, only her words.* The pain could not have disappeared with the mere administration of a gel, but I did not feel it any more. I was moving—very slowly, it is true—but moving nevertheless. With each passing minute, I was getting closer to the finish line, but I realized that only subconsciously; my conscious mind had only one thought—Vinod Ghadge.

Vinod Ghadge had been a sales-tax officer and a champion long-distance swimmer. I had only ever been a sprinter (in the pool), but the swimming community is a small one, and we had

---

*   I learnt later that my never-say-die fellow runner's name was Mala Honnatti and that she was a banker who regularly ran marathons and climbed mountains, both for fun and fitness. In 2015, after having completed the Everest Marathon and the Antarctic Ice Marathon in previous years, she signed up for an Everest expedition, becoming, at sixty-two, the oldest Indian to attempt to summit the world's highest peak. She was mid-climb when the quake that took the lives of twenty-two mountaineers hit the mountain, and was nearly killed herself. That close call hasn't put her off extreme adventuring, though—to this day, she continues to take on difficult challenges, determined not to let fear win.

run into each other enough times to become friends. My admiration for him was not only because of the distances and seas he swam but also because this former cop so often swam for a cause.

I thought about the waters that Vinod had swum, which were some of the roughest patches of sea in the world—four times, as far as I knew, across the 14.4-kilometre-long Strait of Gibraltar, the narrow channel of water connecting the Atlantic Ocean to the Mediterranean Sea, and at least once each across the Palk Strait between India and Sri Lanka (23 kilometres) and across the Toroneos Gulf in Greece (24.5 kilometres). He had also completed the Lake Zurich Marathon Swim, an even longer distance at 26.5 kilometres.

But these huge distances were piffling as far as Vinod was concerned. His favourite stretch of open sea was part of the same shimmering water that lay to my right, a 36.5-kilometre-long patch between the Dharamtar jetty and the Gateway of India. Soon after the horrific events of 26/11, Vinod decided he would swim that route again, this time as a tribute to the victims of Mumbai's worst terrorist attack. His brother Balasaheb and his fifteen-year-old protégé, Dhananjay Kolatkar, would accompany him on the crossing.

Vinod had regularly swum a distance of 36 kilometres. I had tried running 42, and collapsed at 37. I could not help cracking a smile at that.

Impatient as ever, Vinod wanted to do the swim in early December itself, but the navy and the Mumbai Port Trust, *still jittery in the aftermath of the terror that had come via the sea, dithered for weeks over the permission. It was eventually granted just a little over two weeks previously, on the morning of 29 December. Delighted, Vinod decided the trio would swim the tribute that very night—there was no knowing when the permission would be withdrawn again.*

Accompanied by a group of forty well-wishers, including his own wife and children, who would provide support in accompanying boats, the three swimmers set off by road to Dharamtar. At 2 a.m. sharp, Balasaheb and Dhananjay kicked off from the jetty. Vinod followed at 2.20 a.m., allowing the less-experienced, less-speedy ones a head start. He would comfortably catch up with them by the halfway point.

I had no idea how I had made it here, but my beaten legs had nevertheless turned left, off Marine Drive, at Brabourne Stadium. I was back in the Fort area, and there were less than 1.5 kilometres to go. There were so many people on these streets, the noise and colour at fever pitch. People were calling my name a lot more now, cheering me on, urging me to keep moving. The finish line was in sight, and I had left the sea behind, but the sea was still surging inside my head—I could not wish it away.

Around 4.30 a.m. on 30 December, near the Karanjata jetty off the coast of Uran, my friend Vinod Ghadge had run slam-bang into a fishing net. The other two had gone safely over, but Vinod hadn't spotted the buoys in the dark. Hopelessly entangled, he had thrashed and flailed in vain, staying below the surface until it was too late.

I had been running for 4 hours 47 minutes and 44 seconds when I crossed the finish line, a full sixty-two minutes past my original target. People were patting my back, shaking my hand, telling me what a grand job I had done. Reporters, eager for sound bites, surrounded me, asking me how I was feeling at my achievement, why I had taken so long to complete the course, how I had managed to keep running when my entire body was in agony. I answered as best I could, trying to smile and keep it together when I really wanted to be somewhere else, far away, alone with my thoughts.

'Milind,' said a young reporter, thrusting her mic in my face, 'you had said a week ago that you were dedicating this run to Vinod Ghadge, who died attempting a tribute to the 26/11 victims. Is there a message you want to send out to his family?'

All my composure came crashing down. A sea of emotions crashed into me, washing away all my barriers, stripping away all my defences, reducing me to my rawest, most vulnerable state. As the television cameras zoomed in on my face, the tears began to flow.

6

ON THE RUN

'It is strange how new and unexpected conditions bring out unguessed ability to meet them.'

—Edgar Rice Burroughs, *The Warlord of Mars*

As crazy as it sounds, just three weeks after I had completed the Mumbai Marathon, which I still consider one of the toughest runs of my life, I was back on the streets of Bombay, running (told you I was obsessive!). The thing was, once I had recovered from the bruising—physical, mental, emotional—I had received on the marathon trail, I realized that I had learnt so much about what it took to be a long-distance runner in those five hours that it would be a shame not to put those lessons to the test—by running some more.

So here I was, in February, attempting to run 60 kilometres through the city over a twenty-four-hour period. This time, I was running for a cause, as part of NDTV's very first Greenathon, an initiative through which they hoped not only to raise awareness about environmental issues but also raise money—celebrity pledges mainly—for the Tata Energy Research Institute's (TERI) 'Light a Life' campaign. The money would enable TERI to light up sun-drenched villages across the country by night, with the solar-powered lanterns they had developed in-house. With every kilometre I ran, I would personally raise Rs 50,000 for Light a Life. How could I not be a part of it?

It was such a huge high to raise Rs 30 lakh (enough money to light up about seventeen villages) for a worthy cause, simply by pushing my own body, that I was instantly hooked. For Greenathon 2, in 2010, I set myself a bigger challenge—100 kilometres in a twenty-four-hour period—and completed it, raising Rs 50 lakh. It felt great! The next year, I told myself, I would attempt something SERIOUSLY big—I would challenge myself not only to accomplish a much greater feat of endurance, but also, through it, to run a more sustained green campaign and raise a much larger amount of money.

I let that thought marinate for a bit, until, a couple of months later, the Big Idea dropped. Maybe it was the thought of Gandhiji's Dandi March, which he had set out on from the Sabarmati Ashram in Ahmedabad, that triggered it, but I decided that my contribution to Greenathon 3 would be a 550-kilometre-long run. Covering an average distance of 35 kilometres each day, I would run from Ahmedabad to Bombay in fifteen days.

It was a good thing I began thinking big a year before the next Greenathon, because NDTV, delighted by the success of the first two editions, was thinking gigantic. Bollywood stars like Shah Rukh Khan had been part of the campaign from the very first year, each adopting one or more villages to light up, and many more had come on board in 2010, giving NDTV the confidence to change the game entirely. They decided to go international with Greenathon 3, and to add more muscle to their green message and sync it with the rest of the world, they linked it with World Environment Day. That, of course, meant that instead of doing my 556-kilometre run in cool February–March, I was going to have to do it in May–June, under a scorching summer sun. Thanks, guys!

There was no way out now—even if the announcement about the Ahmedabad–Bombay run had not yet been made. I had personally decided to do it, and I can be pretty silly about these things. The body could be prepped, it was the mind that needed tackling. Rather than seeing the summer run as a negative, I convinced myself that the shifting of the Greenathon date to June was an advantage—I now had more time to train for it. Of course, the prep would be punishing, but I was determined to ensure it wasn't all-consuming. I had a full life outside of running, and I wasn't going to compromise on it.

As Greenathon 3 approached, I stepped up my preparation. NDTV did their bit, creating my Twitter handle— @milindrunning—for me in May 2011, introducing me to social media and social media to me for the very first time. It was a revelation. I had no idea that so many people still knew who I was and were interested in hearing about the random things I occupied myself with.

It seems a weird thing to say now, but until I got on to Twitter, I really had no idea how much of a celebrity I was. I'll tell you why. In the early nineties, when my face had become familiar to people through magazines and billboards, I knew I was somewhat famous in Bombay and Delhi because of the coverage I got in the fashion and glamour press. But there was no live-streaming then of fashion shows or events, and with television itself being fairly new, my reach was limited. Even the public reaction to the Tuff shoes ad, which everyone remembers as a big, big deal, didn't really affect me in the way that such a thing would affect even the most minor celebrity now—there were no 24/7 news channels tracking every twist and turn in the controversy, interviewing the woman on the street about her opinion of our lack of morals, or putting together high-powered panels in which everyone yelled at each other about the topic 'Is India seeing the death of creative freedom?' or 'Can Indian *sanskaar* stand up to the onslaught of Western liberal ideas?'

There were no faceless Internet trolls abusing me and Madhu, either. Sure, we had a sense that we were dealing with a bit of a Frankenstein's monster when people took us to court, but we couldn't really tell how many regular people really cared about it, and how much.

Television was a game changer to some extent. With 'Made in India' airing (over and over and over again) on Channel V, a lot more people began to recognize my face. *Captain Vyom*, which aired on the channel with the biggest reach, Doordarshan, made me popular with a different generation and a different demographic, but once again, this is a recent discovery. I never realized at that time how many children were actually watching it or what they felt about it—there was never any occasion for me to meet my young fans. My life consisted of going to the studios, giving my shots and returning home. Of course you knew from what your producer told you that the series was doing well, but there was no way you could guess at the extent.

And then I became an actor in Bollywood, which isolated me even more from people—since I was never one of the leads, I was never involved in the promo tours or press conferences or magazine covers or features. By 2011, it had been over a decade since I had partied or socialized with the glam set, so I never made Page 3, either. As far as I was concerned, I had dropped off the public radar almost entirely, so I assumed that while there must be a few people (almost all of them women) of my generation or younger who still held a candle for me, many people wouldn't even recognize me if I walked past.

In short, by 2011, I was no longer the news, and that suited me fine, since I had actively worked towards that for many years. I have always hated attention—I don't know how to react to it, or what to do with it. I grew up in a time and in a home where access to mirrors was limited, despite the four women I lived with (or perhaps because of it, but I rather think the former). I don't remember my mum or sisters spending much time in front of a mirror at all, or caring so much about clothes—we were a family of academics, where other things were always considered more important than looking good or dressing well. (And yet, the world considered us easy on the eye—once I had started modelling, my sisters got offers to model as well; they all flatly refused.)

It's the universe's ultimate joke on me that for the last thirty years of my life, few conversations that I've had with strangers have ever happened without some reference to my looks, despite all I've done not to highlight them—I rarely dress in anything but a tee and tracks, I don't colour my hair, I run like a crazy man in the Indian sun, with no sunblock on. And if I happen to say to someone that appearances don't count for much, they will almost always retort, 'That's easy for YOU to say.' Then they will ask to take a selfie with me.

The selfie—what *is* with that? In my days as a model, it required so many talented people—stylists, designers, fashion photographers—and so much equipment, to get a good picture. Today, with the combination of social media, fantastic phone cameras and the selfie culture, everyone is a model, everyone's a star. People are looking at themselves constantly, absolutely *obsessing* about their appearance! No one, not even the great Steve Jobs himself, could have predicted, when he demonstrated the front-facing camera on the iPhone 4 in 2010 by making the first FaceTime call, that a feature meant to help businesspeople conduct meetings while on the move would turn into something that would blow the lid off humanity's unbounded vanity. I'm so grateful that I was young in a different time—if I was twenty now and part of the glamour industry, I would never have been able to deal with putting my face out in public constantly, comparing the number of likes I got with how much a fellow model got, teetering day after day on the edge of 'social media depression'.

At fifty-four, of course, I have far fewer hang-ups—I have no problem putting a picture out on my social media accounts every few days. Most of them are selfies, usually taken after a long run, with my hair all over the place and my face nice and sweaty. I still get uneasy when people approach me for a selfie, though, because that means I have to have a conversation with them, and I have never been good at small talk. I have found a way around that, however. I insist they must earn their selfie, by doing push-ups (ten if it is a woman who's asking, twenty for a man). People are a little thrown when I insist—they think I'm joking at first. There's a lot of back and forth—that takes care of the conversation part—until they either do the push-ups and take the selfie, or shake hands with me and leave. Clever, huh?

Of course there are people who get very offended that I'm asking them to *do* something for a selfie. Especially because I insist on push-ups in situ, as it were—it doesn't matter whether we are in the lobby of a five-star hotel or next to a roadside chai shop, they have to do it right there. 'Who does he think he is?' said one indignant senior citizen in Kathmandu about my demand. 'He expects women to prostrate at his feet!' Of course I do not. I just think that if I have become the country's poster boy for an active lifestyle and 24/7 fitness, I have to promote that idea as well, one woman—or man—at a time. The good part is that, even if the person who has approached me goes away without having done the push-ups, I have had a conversation with them about what I believe in, and that's fantastic. Whether they agree with me or not, they will talk about the interaction to their friends, and the message will go even further. That's a win as far as I am concerned.

~

When I was introduced to social media in 2011 by NDTV, the selfie hadn't been named that yet. I was on Twitter, which hadn't yet rolled out its photo-sharing feature. Twitter was words, and I have always been comfortable with words. What was even better was that I didn't have to tweet about myself. Sure, I would be chronicling my run on Twitter on a daily basis, but that run was not so much about me as it was about the cause of the environment, another thing I have always been passionate about. I had no shyness, no coyness, about sending out messages, even several messages a day, about that. The reach of the medium was clearly tremendous and broke through all demographic and cultural barriers, but what made it even more exciting for me was that it was direct—every person who saw the tweet could believe that the message was for them alone, and react to it as an individual. I loved it!

I kicked off my mega intercity run with a five-member team of runners—Raj, Mahesh, Apurba, Sohanlal and Sajjan—on 22 May 2011. My first-ever tweet went out on 23 May and set the context: 'Started the Green Run from

Ahmedabad to Bombay yesterday / 550 km in 15 days. Weather fantastic 40 degrees in the shade. ☺'

Later that same evening, another tweet went out: 'Blisters. I've never had those before.'

As you can imagine, the blisters only got worse as the days rolled by, but each day brought new insights about the western countryside and introduced us to all the tremendous local initiatives geared towards protecting the environment. Most of these were sustained simply by love and passion, with no government or organizational support at all. Being on Twitter—and on TV, doing a live report for NDTV each night—gave me the opportunity to spread the word about these initiatives for fifteen days running (haha). It (almost) made all the pain and the effort worthwhile.

To those who read about it, and to most people we met on the way, a 550-kilometre run seemed like an insane, superhuman, even pointless, enterprise. But for me, personally, it was none of those things at all—my body had been well-conditioned, and each day brought interactions that were so inspiring that my spirit was consistently buoyant. There was occasional despair, though. One of my tweets, somewhere along the way, reads: 'I wish I could pretend I was passing through beautiful Indian towns, but I'm not.' At the end of the fortnight, though, blisters or not, the run was successfully completed. In fact, Greenathon 3 was a mega success as a whole, raising over Rs 11 crore for 'Light a Life'.

Predictably, I did not rest on my laurels. I was now itching to chase something even bigger, something so audacious that it would make the country sit up and take notice. When the idea took root and blossomed, it even surprised me with its scale and scope—in double the time it had taken me to run from Ahmedabad to Bombay, I would attempt to run triple the distance. In thirty days, covering an average of 50 kilometres a day, I would run the 1500-kilometre distance between Delhi and Bombay.

Everyone baulked a bit at that, but I had my mind made up. I picked my team—a bunch of five runners, including a woman, all of them as insane as I—and began to prepare for the coming ordeal. As a concession to the extreme heat, we decided to start our run in mid-April (20 April 2012, to be precise) rather than early May, even if it meant that we would finish on 20 May, well before World Environment Day. We would kick off at the Qutub Minar in Delhi and end at the Yash Raj Films studios in Andheri, Bombay.

What is the best way to describe a thirty-day run that got my five teammates and me into the *Limca Book of Records*? Does the fact that I lost a total of seven kilos and five toenails in the duration give you an idea of what it was like? Does it help you see it better if I tell you that on Day 14, I was laid low by a sharp and very, very severe pain in my glutes that did not bother me so much when I was upright but was excruciating when I attempted to sit or lie down? PS: It never went away for the next sixteen days and immobilized me partially for months after, besides creating such severe mental stress both during and after the run that I thought I would never recover from it.

Can you imagine the monotony of running nine to ten hours each day in the blazing sun, between 4 a.m. and 7 p.m., never sure of what kind of food was available on the way (we did not have a cook travelling with us), hoping against hope that we would pass close enough to a lake to dive in for a quick, refreshing swim, but never finding it? Could you begin to understand what it was like if I told you that it was, physically and mentally, my toughest-ever challenge, that I came very, very close to quitting, many, many times?

Maybe there are some experiences that cannot be described at all, except in the most clichéd terms, but if I had to pick just one word, it would be *traumatic*.

Through the thirty days, my team and I, while we were there for each other throughout, while we high-fived at the end of each day and fist-bumped before we set off each morning, never actually talked to each other about how we were feeling. It was as if we had reached some kind of tacit agreement never to discuss what we were going through or the personal demons we were battling inside our heads; it was as if each of us feared, and understood, that sharing our pain and our doubts would disturb our focus and make us weak, and none of us wanted that. Holding it all in was a kind of penance in itself, making us stronger each day—by never discussing it, we ensured that the 1500-kilometre goal remained a non-negotiable one. We had made a covenant with each other, the country and Mother Nature, and we would fulfil it if it killed us.

It almost did. If it did not quite kill me, the pain in my glutes certainly put me out of commission for weeks and weeks after. The first doctor I saw ordered tests, diagnosed my condition as a slipped disc and told me to stay in bed for two weeks straight. But lying in bed was no party—no position was comfortable, and I was constantly shifting from lying flat on my back to lying on my side to lying on my stomach. The worst bit was that even all that rest wasn't helping much. Much later, I would find out that not working your muscles for more than two days at a stretch is actually detrimental. Muscles are meant to be used, they need to be flexed and extended often and regularly to keep them in good fettle. A two-week resting period, while it may be inevitable in some cases, is never a good idea for an otherwise healthy person. My only big win from that period was a return to reading— in those fifteen days, I started and finished the entire *Game of Thrones* series.

Slightly recovered from that extended period of rest, I returned to my regular life. Only to be felled again, and again, by the same pain in my glutes. Nothing that any doctor recommended seemed to have a lasting effect. In December,

I gave up on the doctors and surrendered, very sceptically, to the ministrations of a young female physiotherapist who had impressed me with her confidence. In the beginning, she reckoned that what I had was scoliosis, an abnormal curvature of the spine, but when she had taken a closer look, she changed her diagnosis completely, insisting it was a muscle spasm, a bad one, but nothing that a deep-tissue massage of my buttocks could not cure. Do you blame me for being sceptical?

As it turned out, she was more than right. After my first appointment, just ten minutes into the massage, the pain was gone, completely, and as I was to find out, permanently. It was nothing short of miraculous.

I discovered later that what I had had was a common neuromuscular disorder called the 'piriformis syndrome', where the piriformis muscle compresses the sciatic nerve. It is a condition that affects people who engage in vigorous activities that cause repetitive trauma to the area, people like—ta-da!—long-distance runners. In January 2013, a little over a month after my miracle cure, I comfortably ran the Mumbai Marathon.

I have never been a happy pill-popper, believing that the body has the tools to heal itself, given time and rest and nutrition, but I am now a big fan of physiotherapy—that, I believe, is the kind of external help the body could definitely benefit from.

The 1500-kilometre 'mindathon' also taught me a lot about running and about setting oneself audacious goals. It showed me, with blinding clarity, that you never know what you are truly capable of until you try. It reinforced my belief that there is no such thing as failure when you push yourself to attempt something new and 'impossible', for each day brings fresh learning, each experience insight, perspective, wisdom. To my mind, that is the ultimate win.

~

'To me there always seems a way to gain the opposite side of an obstacle. If one cannot pass over it, or below it, or around it, why then there is but a single alternative left, and that is to pass through it.'

—Edgar Rice Burroughs, *John Carter: Adventures on Mars*

What next? Would I run the distance from Kashmir to Kanyakumari? I could have tried that, I suppose, I still may some day, but I didn't see any sense in doing more of the same. Not yet, anyway—for now, I needed a different challenge, something that would help me engage with the community at large, solve a social problem, take me beyond myself; all the inspiring people I'd met on the way had seen to that. I had been tossing an idea around in my head for the past couple of years, and it seemed to me that its time had come.

Why do people become entrepreneurs? What would be your motivation for starting a company of your own? Everyone has different triggers, I suppose, but I start businesses mainly for one reason—I love the challenge of turning an idea that engages my mind into a sustainable enterprise. I come from a family of professionals, not businessmen—I have no inherited business skills. I don't see a business as something that should make me a lot of money, but as something that gives me an opportunity to explore an idea while it supports itself and pays the salaries of all the people involved. This was my philosophy when I started my first business in 1989, and it continues to be my philosophy thirty years later. (Let that be a lesson to you, boys and girls, it's never too early, or too late, to start your own business!)

Here's a little side note. There is a question I am asked so often that it will be definitely part of the FAQs on my website, if I ever have one—*If you keep running all the time, how do you earn a living, man?* There are variants of this— when I tell people they should run, swim, cycle, move every single day, they often come back with, 'Easy for you to say. You don't have to go to work each day like we do.'

Right. Here are my responses. To the question about how I make a living, the answer is that the money, or some of it, at any rate, comes from all the businesses I'm part of. And some of it comes from speaking about health and fitness. As for the second part, I do go to work each day, just like everyone else; the difference is that I work for myself. (The fact that you work long hours for someone else isn't a good enough excuse for you not to make fitness part of your life, by the way. You can, and should, always find time for the things you consider important, and there's nothing more important than your health. In fact, because of my own lack of time, I have created a daily workout that is only three minutes long and works very well for me. Burn that into your brain.)

But back to the idea I had been toying around with. For some years now, every time I participated in a marathon or any kind of run, I had noticed that the percentage of women running was minuscule compared to men. I wondered about that, and began to ask people why that was so. I got different answers, but most people seemed to think that it was because Indian women were simply not interested in running. Actually, I was told over and over again, they are not interested in sport of any kind—how many girls do you see on the street playing cricket or watching a football match on TV?

Coming from a family of women who took fitness seriously, I wasn't entirely convinced. I knew from personal experience that one of the biggest reasons that women in general, and Indian women in particular, don't exercise, is the guilt they feel for taking time away from their families. It is only when they have made sure that their husbands and children and parents and in-laws have been taken care of, that they even begin to think about themselves, and by then they are too tired. To take time out on a Sunday morning, which was sacred 'family time', to run with hundreds of strangers, many of them men (and who knew what kind of men they were?), wearing the kind of clothes they were not used to wearing, was not likely to be at the top of their list of priorities. Add to that the fact that they would have to take time out to train before the event, and the idea was dead in the water.

Of course, my theories were purely anecdotal, but if what I believed was true, it was a serious concern. It was mums who held families together, who fashioned the subtle rules of engagement between family members and the world. It was they who decided what the family ate and when, and they who, by simply living their lives, set examples, both good and bad, for their children to imbibe. Empowered women set the best kind of example to their children, and the first step towards empowerment, for a woman, was to take charge of her own health, respect herself and understand and celebrate the value she brought to her family and to society.

If women began to take an interest in their fitness, if they took it seriously and talked about it and showed, in a million little ways, that it was important to them, everyone else in the family would follow suit, and we would have a healthier society, a fitter nation. If, on the other hand, women didn't think it counted for much—or believed it did but did nothing about it—their children, taking the cue, would also end up not thinking of fitness as an important life-goal.

It was so simple if you looked at it that way—get the women out of their homes, get them moving, get them fit, and you have the beginnings of a country-wide fitness and empowerment revolution. It was a mind-blowingly exciting prospect—how could I not take a punt at it?

I had been thinking about hosting a women-only run for a while now and had been talking about it to my partner at Maximus Events, Reema Sanghavi. Like everyone else, she had been sceptical, believing it would be a very small event and not worth our while. I had been busy myself, so I had let it slide all these months, but in the weeks after the Green Run, the idea returned to haunt me. Because it was at the top of my mind, I mentioned it to journalist Malavika Sangghvi, who got very excited and wanted to write about it. I considered—it was one way to force Reema's hand, and mine. 'Sure,' I said, 'we will announce it at a press conference next month.' Then I went to Reema and presented the Women's Run as a fait accompli, putting her into a real flap. I do that a lot.

In October 2012, at a well-attended press conference, Reema, Bipasha Basu and I announced the very first Women's

Run in Bombay. In keeping with my business philosophy, I had decided that we would only raise sponsorships; we would not ask for donations, for a women's run did not need charity. The idea was to get so many women running that sponsors would beg to pour their money into the event. Our run would be called the Pinkathon, and it was meant to raise awareness about breast cancer, while urging women to get fit. The message was that running was a great way to keep your body in top condition, and since a fit body had a better immune system, it also had a better chance of fighting any disease, including cancer.

The first Pinkathon—if too few people showed up, it would be the only Pinkathon—was slated to happen in Bombay on 16 December. So as to not intimidate potential participants, the longest run category had been fixed at 10 kilometres. There were also going to be shorter runs— 3 kilometres and 5 kilometres—and there would be pre-announced practice runs, training sessions and a lot more in the weeks leading up to the event. Having made the announcement it, we sat back and waited, fingers tightly crossed.

The response was stupendous. Women all over the city loved the idea of doing something only for themselves, in a safe space, surrounded by other women. Social media was abuzz, radio jockeys got involved, there was a tremendous amount of excitement. Meanwhile, I got busy assembling star power for the occasion—Karisma Kapoor agreed to flag off the event, and Lisa Hayden, Tara Sharma, Anusha Dandekar and Gul Panag would be there to show support, along with my old friend, Devika Bhojwani, a cancer survivor herself. Needless to say, my fit-as-a-fiddle Aai, never one to miss an occasion like this, would not only be there but also join the run herself.

On 16 December 2012, to our great delight, we had over 2000 highly enthusiastic, highly motivated women turn up to run, not for prizes, not for recognition, but for the simple joy of being with a whole lot of other women, all committed to doing something for themselves for the first time.

Given the amount of effort that had gone into organizing it, 2000 wasn't a very large number of participants, but it was large enough for a debut outing—it showed us, unequivocally, that we were on to something. By the time the day was done, though, the numbers had become incidental—we had experienced for ourselves, as had each of those 2000 women, the tremendous positive vibe that came from so many happy women being in one place together—dancing, cheering, hugging and, of course, running. This, we realized, was big. This was important. This simply had to be grown. That day, Reema became even more committed than I was to the idea of Pinkathon. We decided to go national with it, and quickly.

We rolled out Pinkathon in four cities in 2013—Bangalore came first, in April, with an incredible 3500 women participating; Delhi in September; Pune in November; and Bombay, for the second time, in December. But even before we came back to Bombay, Pinkathon had created such positive word-of-mouth influence on the women's grapevine across the country that other cities began to clamour for their own Pinkathon. That would be beyond our bandwidth, but I didn't want to disappoint anyone, so we created an event called Megapink—on one specific date in November, women in as many cities as were interested would run together for breast-cancer awareness, for health and fitness, and for joy.

All it took was an announcement on my Facebook page—oh yes, in 2012, I had gotten on to FB, just to promote Pinkathon—for women in thirty-five cities across the country to volunteer to organize the Megapink run in their hometowns. In an unbelievably short time, we had printed our signature pink-and-white T-shirts for every runner. Shipping them out was going to be expensive, but for the sense of solidarity we were hoping to create among the women who were running, the T-shirts were very important—it had to be done. On the day we were to begin shipping, Blue Dart came on board, offering to ship all the boxes out to all thirty-five cities for free! I was on a perpetual high that year—I could not believe I had created this powerful idea around which so many women, men and corporates were rallying, sometimes even without being asked.

In 2014, Pinkathon went to six cities, in 2015 to eight; we have now capped it at that number. We have even had to cap the number of participants in each city—Delhi, Bombay and Bangalore are capped at 11k, and fill up the quickest, while Pune, Hyderabad, Chennai, Kolkata and Guwahati are getting there. A large number of people in each city began to help spread the message of Pinkathon and became ambassadors to the cause. Because of their incredible enthusiasm, in 2018, we drew up blueprints for an annual Pinkathon Day on the lines of Megapink (which, inexplicably, we never ran after 2013) and announced the date a couple of months earlier.

Once again, the response was unbelievable: on 21 October, Pinkathon Day 2018, women in 130 locations across sixty-three cities and six countries—the Maldives, the UK, the USA, Dubai, Nepal and Singapore, besides India—ran to celebrate 'har ghar mein Pinkathon'—the idea that if every woman in the family realised the value of an active lifestyle, it would lead to a fitter family, a fitter society and a fitter India. In 2019, the numbers were bigger—we had 176 locations across ten countries spread across Asia, North America, Europe and Africa, registered for the Pinkathon Day Run on 20 October 2019, with more than 25,000 participants.

Pinkathon was never conceived of as just a race, and it has never been just that. From its inception, it has been a community project to spread awareness about the benefits of an active lifestyle for women, and that has been its guiding principle these last seven years. Each year, it has added new and exciting facets to itself—the 21k distance, the free mammogram for every participant over forty-five, the free registration for the house help (every participant can register her house help along with herself, for free—that way, the message of women's health reaches new audiences, and an economically disadvantaged woman gets the benefit of a free mammogram), the we-run-in-saris/hijabs brigades, the moms-who-run set (who run with their babies strapped to their chests or backs), the visually impaired and hearing-impaired girls-who-run, and so much more.

But perhaps its biggest achievement has been to eliminate the guilt women feel about taking time out for themselves—when they see thousands of women like themselves congregating in the wee hours of the morning, dancing to peppy music as they warm up, having themselves a very good time, it makes them feel that it is not only okay to be away from their families, but vitally important.

Oh, and Pinkathon now also has a mascot, the amazing, amazing Mann Kaur of Patiala, who, at the age of 104, is the reigning world champion in her age category in the 100 and 200 metres sprint and the javelin and shot put throw—she broke her own previous record in the 100 metres sprint at the World Masters Championships in 2017, running the distance in 1 minute 14 seconds!

Because I founded Pinkathon, I am often hailed as a feminist or extolled as an activist for women's health and fitness. I also—sigh—get trolled for having chosen breast-cancer awareness as a goal, over awareness of some other lesser-known but equally fatal feminine diseases. Let me clear the air on both these statements right now. I did not create Pinkathon because I cared deeply about women in general or because I believe in gender equality (I do, but that is not the reason I created the run). I did it because I noticed that there were very few women running, and to me, that was an intellectual problem begging to be solved. I chose breast-cancer awareness not because it was 'trending' or because I wanted to take the easy way out with a disease whose PR was already in place, but because one in twenty-two Indian women contract the disease, and early screening and awareness—and an active lifestyle—can actually help save lives.

There was another problem that I believed needed solving—there was hardly any athleisure wear specifically designed for the Indian woman. There was no fitness fashion line that was trendy while being modest, loved Indian body shapes but did not hug them too closely and was, in general, more in keeping with the silhouettes Indian women were used to. I already had designs in mind—comfortable dhoti and harem pants, 'skeggings' (leggings that have a skirt attached at the top, to hide big butts), longer tees in a soft, natural material that didn't cling. I was also very clear that all the clothes had to be made in the most sustainable, ethical way as far as the environment was concerned. In 2016, I joined hands with sports business entrepreneur Darshan M to create the athleisure brand Deivee—skeggings are no longer just a figment of my imagination.

In fact, even though the idea for Pinkathon came from me, and it was Reema and I who created it, I hate talking about the event as 'mine'. It is for that reason that you will never see my face on any Pinkathon poster or hoarding or any other collateral—the movement is not about me at all. With over 65,000 women, 70 per cent of whom are first-timers, running across eight cities each year, Pinkathon is today India's biggest women's run. It has grown way bigger, and way more powerful, than the original idea or persons behind it. And that is exactly as it should be.

~

'But the girl, ah—that was a different matter. He did not reason here. He knew that she was created to be protected, and that he was created to protect her.'

—Edgar Rice Burroughs, *Tarzan of the Apes*

While Pinkathon was growing and flourishing like the green bay tree, quite a lot was happening in my other lives. The most important one of them all happened in the nightclub of an upscale Chennai hotel towards the end of February 2014, a month and some before the inaugural Chennai Pinkathon was due to be flagged off.

Just so you understand, this is how Pinkathon set-ups work—six weeks before the event, the Maximus team arrives in the city. They hole up in a hotel for the next forty-five days, liaising with local officials and police, getting permissions, identifying and working with local vendors for a variety of products and services, ironing out any last-minute kinks that crop up, and basically getting things absolutely right—or as right as one can get them—for the actual event. Such a set-up was in progress in Chennai at the end of February, and I happened to be around as well.

I had stayed at the hotel where my team was staying several times before. Each time, the manager had requested me to put in a 'celebrity appearance' at the hotel's nightclub, and each time, I had managed to slip away with some thinly disguised excuse. That particular day—it was a Thursday, and ladies' night at the club—he caught me at the reception and made his request again. I could see my team looking at me hopefully—they really wanted to go, but they couldn't unless I went too. What the heck, I thought to myself, I'll just hang around for fifteen minutes, do a bit of dancing and leave—aren't celebrities supposed to do that?

So I went into a nightclub after God knows how many years, and as before, the women began to swarm around me, asking for a dance. I had been dancing for a bit when I looked across the room and saw a girl staring hard at me. She is the cutest thing in here, I remember thinking, if I had to choose to get to know one person in the room, I would pick her. So while I was too busy to actively seek a new relationship, I wasn't averse to one if it happened serendipitously, with the right person.

Allow me to take a brief time-out here to clarify something. Whatever one may say about me, one thing that cannot be said is that I am some kind of predatory Casanova. As I have said before, I have been deeply committed to all the relationships I have been in, for as long as they have lasted. Sure, I've done things as a young man that I am not proud of, but as I grew older, I learned to value all relationships more. Whenever I've been between relationships, there has never been a lack of beautiful, accomplished women trying to get my attention, but I'm not, nor have ever been, into the one-night stand. As for dating women much younger than me, let's just say that, for me, whether we are talking fitness or relationships, age is just a number.

I continued dancing, my eyes searching for the girl every few minutes, but she had moved away—I couldn't spot her anywhere. I turned to leave, and there she was, right in front of me, looking straight at me. I could see that her friend was pushing her towards me, propping her up from the back. 'Hello,' she said, 'would you like to dance?' Would I! 'Why not,' I said.

Now, I remember this dance lasting three or four song-lengths, but Ankita insists it lasted forty-five minutes, or ten song-lengths. I wouldn't take her word for it, though, and neither should you—she and her friends had had way too much to drink by then. She also remembers me asking the most inane questions: Where was she from? What did her father do? How many siblings did she have? What did she do for a living?

She was more than a little annoyed—here she was, dancing with this hunk called Milind Soman, who she had a serious crush on, and he was being so spectacularly boring! After fifteen minutes (or forty-five), she told me she was just going to step out for a smoke. 'You smoke?' I said, sounding as righteously indignant as I felt. 'You don't?' she retorted. 'N-o,' I said, suddenly not feeling so virtuous—or cool!—any more, to her retreating back.

I continued dancing with anyone else who wanted a dance, waiting for her to return. But she never did, or at least not for the next thirty minutes. I walked over to her friends and asked where she was. I wasn't sure if they even understood what I was saying—they looked totally spaced out—but one of them evidently did; she went and found her. 'Where have you been?' I demanded. 'I told you I was going out for a smoke!' she said indignantly. 'How long does that take?' I said. 'I've been waiting all this while for you.' She looked at me really strangely then, wondering what she had got herself into. 'But I never asked you to wait for me!' she snapped, forcing me on to the back foot. 'Oh all right,' I retreated quickly. 'I just wanted to say bye. I'm leaving for Bombay tomorrow.' She shrugged. 'See you around.'

I was stumped. Did this girl not know anything? What kind of twenty-two-year-old did not recognize an opening line when she heard one? I would have to go direct with this one, and deal with whatever came after. 'Give me your phone number,' I said. 'I'd like to keep in touch.'

'Oh,' she said, 'I've just got my India phone, and I don't remember my number.' Christ! This girl seemed determined to shuck off every shred of self-respect I still had left. 'Well, take *my* number then,' I said. 'I'm not carrying my phone,' she replied. I had just about had it. I called one of her friends over and gave him my phone number. 'Give it to her later tonight,' I said, 'when she is reunited with her phone.' And I turned on my heel and left.

I rose early the next morning, as always, and quickly checked my phone. No message from the cute girl. Oh well. It was much later, around 9.30 a.m., that the message I had been waiting for came. *I had a lovely time last evening,* she wrote. *Thank you.* My heart leapt. *Join me for breakfast?* I texted back quickly. *Sorry,* she said, *I'm already on my way to work.* She had told me the previous night that she worked at the airport—she had just come back into India from Malaysia, where she had been working, to set up her airline's India operations—so I left a little early to catch my flight, hoping to see her there. *I'm at the airport,* I texted when I got there. *Join me for lunch?* No go. *I'm so sorry, I can't really leave my workstation right now.*

Luckily, like the Pinkathon team, Ankita and her colleagues were also staying at the Chennai hotel for several weeks. When I went back to Chennai a fortnight later, she finally agreed to join me for dinner. We think of that dinner now as our first date.

When I joined Instagram later that year, I put a picture of her up as one of my very first posts, with the cryptic caption 'Isengfa ☺'. People have asked about that for a while, and I can reveal the answer here—Isengfa is Ankita's Ahom, or traditional Assamese, name.

Ankita and I kept our relationship under wraps for the next couple of years, not in an obsessively secretive kind of way, but just by not talking about it in public forums or on social media (Oh, all right, apart from that one Instagram post). Aai, my sisters and Ankita's parents knew about it, though, as did a few close friends. Marriage itself was not on the cards, had never been—when we had first started dating, I had told her quite clearly that I was not interested in marriage, and she had happily concurred, expressing her own extreme distaste for it. With that big elephant out of the way, we settled into a wonderful and mutually rewarding relationship, which, needless to say, also involved a lot of running. Luckily for me, she had been deeply into sport herself as a girl and was more than up to the challenge.

But Ankita was fragile in other ways. As we spent more time together and she learnt to trust me, I found out that she had lost her boyfriend in a bike accident three years previously. That devastating event had sent her reeling into a downward spiral—she had fallen into all kinds of addictions and struggled often with severe bouts of depression. It fell to me to make her see what the good life, la dolce vita, was all about, and nudge her back into it. It would be a long time before she healed, but she was a great student, with a fierce determination and will. Together, through a combination of running, yoga, meditation and lots of love, we slowly and steadily got her healthy again, in body, mind and spirit.

~

'But life would be very miserable indeed were I to spend it in terror of the thing that has not yet happened.'

—Edgar Rice Burroughs, *The Son of Tarzan*

The other big—and, in a way life-changing—event also happened in 2014. One of the 'Pinkathon ambassadors'—we have them in all cities where the Pinkathon is run—had invited me to flag off a running event of some kind in Ahmedabad, and I had agreed without checking what exactly the event was about. When I got there, I realized that it was in fact a mini-triathlon—a 200-metre swim, followed by 5 kilometres of cycling and a 2.5-kilometre run. It was so mini that it felt silly to stand by and watch—I wanted to do it too. I hate cycling and never do it if I can help it, but 5 kilometres seemed eminently doable. Everyone loved the idea; I joined the participants and completed the triathlon myself.

Once it was all done, a bunch of us were sitting together, chatting, when Kimberley Shah, an American triathlete and coach who is now settled in India, suggested that I try my hand at a proper triathlon. Since I already had running and swimming down pat, I only needed to figure out my cycling and train to do all of them in the same race. The idea grabbed me. I thought about it for a few weeks, did some research and decided, impulsively, that I would take a shot at the Ironman Triathlon in 2015. There are over three dozen Ironman Triathlons conducted each year across six continents—and the one I zeroed in on was scheduled for July, in Zurich. I reckoned I had enough time—about nine months—to prepare for it. I would be turning fifty in

2015, and completing this triathlon would be a great way to celebrate that milestone.

The Ironman Triathlon is widely considered the world's toughest one-day sporting event. Participants have to complete a 3.86-kilometre swim, a 180.25-kilometre bicycle ride and a full marathon (42.2 kilometres), one after the other, and in that order, in under seventeen hours. To make it even harder, each of these legs has its own cut-off time as well. The men's record in the Ironman is 7 hours 35 minutes, the women's 8 hours 18 minutes. Anu Vaidyanathan became India's first-ever Ironman—yup, India's first Ironman was a woman—in 2009, at the age of twenty-five. The highest number of Ironmen triathletes in India come from the city of—hold your breath—Kolhapur. Anju Khosla is now our oldest—she won her title in July 2018 at the age of fifty-two.

So my decision to try the Ironman was not entirely unprecedented. I messaged Kimberly, asking her to create a training programme for me. Delighted that I had decided to do it, she messaged back immediately, with a thirty-five-hours-a-week training schedule.

Thirty-five hours a week? That would mean five hours a day, seven days a week. There was no way I could find that kind of time. I asked her to draw up another one for me that didn't involve so much time. She came back with a twenty-five-hours-a-week one. Even that was too tall an order. In the end, I designed my own schedule, setting aside fourteen hours a week for training.

By the time I started training, I had only eighty-eight days left. I trained as hard and as well as I could, even though there were several weeks when I could not hit even the much-abbreviated fourteen hours of training. I never lost sight of the big picture, though—I had nothing to prove to anyone and was in this only to challenge myself and see how far I could go. I wasn't looking to set records, I was looking only to complete the course in the sixteen-hour time-frame (the time limit for the Zurich Ironman was 16 hours, not the usual 17; anyone who finishes the course within the given time earns the right to be called an Ironman).

On 19 July, as ready as I would ever be, I swam, cycled and ran the course in Zurich, along with over 2000 other people. The only difference between all the others and me was that I did the entire course . . . in sandals!

When I first let the course directors know what I was planning, they were quick to call me out—the Ironman rules specified clearly that the runner's toes should not be visible, whatever footwear he or she chose to wear. I countered by pleading a 'medical issue', one that made it impossible for me to wear shoes. Conceding that it was a fair plea, the directors asked for a medical certificate attesting to my peculiar 'condition', which I produced. It worked!

As for the race itself, I had no concerns at all about the swim and the run—I'd been doing both for years. The real concern was completing the 180-kilometre cycling leg in eight hours; if I had a flat, it would be difficult to make up for the time lost in changing it. Luckily, the gods were smiling down—I completed the entire run–swim–bike course well within the time limit, in 15 hours 19 minutes. At the age of fifty, I had earned the right to wear the cheeky Ironman T-shirt I had seen someone wearing in Zurich: *You run the marathon? How cute.*

Something changed irrevocably after I had completed my first Ironman. Doubt disappeared, and a huge self-belief, the kind I had never known before, took root. I was inundated with wishes as everyone hailed me for completing one of the world's toughest challenges. When I responded that it was really not all that difficult, and that anyone could do it, people were aghast—they either were indignant that I was belittling the achievements of all the other Indian Ironmen before me (and *with* me—four other Indians completed the Zurich Ironman with me) or became annoyed at what they saw as my attempt at humble brag. But neither had been my intention at all—I was simply speaking the truth. I truly believe that anyone can do the Ironman, or any other challenge that they set themselves—you have only got to believe that it is possible. The body can be made ready for any challenge with proper, regular conditioning—it is the mind that is the weak link. Once that is mastered, anything is possible.

With fear and doubt vaporizing like a mirage on a hot day in the aftermath of the Ironman, I decided, along with my friend Abhishek Mishra, to sign up for the more formidable Ultraman challenge that was to take place in Florida in February 2017.

On paper, the Ultraman is way, way scarier than the Ironman. It is a three-day-long mega triathlon, a gruelling endurance challenge spanning over 517 kilometres, involving, on Day 1, a 10-kilometre swim in open water followed by a 148-kilometre bike ride; on Day 2, a 275-kilometre bike ride; and on Day 3, an 84-kilometre run. All three legs have to be completed in under thirty-six hours. It is so scary-sounding that most people give up simply on finding out what it involves—while between 2000 and 3000 people participate in each of the three dozen Ironman triathlons, with 70 per cent of them completing it successfully, only about forty-five people bother to even sign up for the Ultraman challenge.

But with my new level of self-belief giving me wings, I not only signed up for the Ultraman but also made a decision that would reek of arrogance and sheer chutzpah to anyone who could not see what I was seeing or feel what I was feeling—I decided I would attempt the challenge *without training for it. At all.* That did not mean I would lounge around in bed for the next seven months, no sirree. I would continue to run, swim and cycle regularly until February rolled around, but I would do it as part of my daily fitness and endurance regimen, without making it about the Ultraman.

If you think about it, that is really what endurance training is about, preparing your body every day, every hour, every minute, for all kinds of unexpected challenges—disease, sudden trauma, a never-before physical feat. The body, not knowing what it is being readied for so assiduously, prepares for the worst, the toughest, the most challenging—and that's exactly what you want. In my personal experience, getting the mind involved by setting targets—I want to be 'fit enough' to complete the Ultraman—is actually limiting, detrimental, on many counts. The mind will stress about its target and overthink the process; prompted by the mind, the body will decide how much is 'enough' to meet that particular target and not stretch itself. By allowing your body to do what it does so well by itself, you allow your mind the opportunity to learn from the body's extensive knowledge, which is so much richer, deeper, more instinctive, more intuitive and more connected to the environment than the mind's.

I had been working on this 'take the thinking out of it' experiment in other ways as well in recent years. Since 2011, I had been experimenting with barefoot running as a concept, and over the years, I had become more and more committed to it. I had stopped wearing shoes entirely after I lost five toenails in the 1500-kilometre Green Run of 2012—since then, I had run either in sandals or chappals, or, most often, with no footwear at all. The advantage of running barefoot is that it rekindles ancient connections that our feet have always had with the earth; it reopens neural pathways that have atrophied from long disuse. Reading signals directly from the feet—about the terrain, the topography, the temperature—the body is able to automatically, organically adjust its gait, posture and technique to its surroundings in real time, allowing for the kind of efficient movement that is not always possible with shoes on.

With the Ultraman fast approaching, I decided the time had come to put all my theories and implicit beliefs about preparation to the test. Over three long, exhausting days between 17 and 19 February 2016, I revelled in watching my body cope with every formidable task that was placed before it. My mind, entirely free of anxiety, and of the desire to control and manage the body, was blissfully relaxed. The race itself, however, as expected, was punishing. Here is how it went.

Day 1 was a breeze—I finished the swim and the bike ride comfortably, with over two hours to spare before the deadline. Hey, I remember thinking, that was not so bad! Ha! Little did I know then what a nail-biting killer Day 2 would be. I completed the 284-kilometre bike ride, a twelve-hour insane effort, just five seconds—five seconds!!!—before the deadline, escaping disqualification by the skin of my teeth.

(Disqualification would have been unbearable, considering it would have come after twelve hours of insane effort.) Day 3 was tough again, but not as bad as Day 2—I finished the 84-kilometre run with seven minutes to go. Phew.

34 hours and 46 minutes after the starter's gun had gone off, I crossed the finish line to become an Ultraman.

The four other Indians participating that year—Abhishek Mishra, Kaustubh Radkar, Prithviraj Patil and Manmadh Rebba—also finished comfortably. When the huzzahs began, I had to insist, once again, that the Ultraman was really not that impossible a challenge at all. Once again, I wasn't being modest. How, in all fairness, could I claim that I had accomplished something stupendous when I had been beaten, by hours, by a sixty-seven-year-old man with only one leg?

I thought about how things had changed, how *I* had changed, in the fourteen years since I had started running. At thirty-eight, I had thought finishing a half-marathon would be difficult. At fifty-two, I knew becoming an Ultraman was easy.

~

'So gloriously does love transfigure its object.'

—Edgar Rice Burroughs, *The Return of Tarzan*

Two years after Ankita and I had first started dating, a reporter asked me, during the Guwahati Pinkathon, if I was seeing someone. I nodded yes, adding (rather unnecessarily, now that I think about it) that she was Assamese. All hell broke loose. Local newspapers, tagging me *'Axomor juwai'*—'Assam's son-in-law'—went to town, speculating about the identity of my girlfriend. Ankita's parents were very upset, and the poor girl had her hands full calming them down. They did soon enough, though, when no one managed to trace me back to their daughter.

In early 2017, my athleisure fashion brand Deivee was showing its Spring–Summer '18 collection at the Delhi Fashion Week. Ankita and I were there, and someone managed to take a picture of the two of us holding hands as we walked around the hotel. He or she posted it on social media, tagging it *SS '18*. Some genius decided the 18 in the caption referred to Ankita's age (she was twenty-five at the time), and put that fun 'fact' out into the world. That did it. Howling and baying for my blood, the trolls came out in full force, calling all manner of curses down upon my head for consorting with a girl who was barely legal. They did their research, discovered that I had been dating her for three years and proceeded to completely flip their lids—what kind of a man was I, they demanded, that I would date a fifteen-year-old girl?

Luckily, neither Ankita nor I were too affected by all the toxicity around us. It was shocking how much venom these trolls had to spew, how much hate they carried inside them, for people they did not know at all. Deep inside, though, I understood where their nameless, terrible fear was coming from—the social order that they had been taught to uphold, that they had protected, believed in and lived by so fiercely, was crumbling around them. If they allowed one person to get away with such a blatant flouting of social norms without protesting with all their might, what was to prevent more people—their own sons and daughters, for instance—from doing the same?

Now that her name was out in print, Ankita's parents, the Konwars, began to get extremely jittery. But their elder daughter's wedding was occupying their entire headspace at the time, so they let us be for a bit. After the wedding, Ankita—yes, the same girl that had once turned up her pretty nose at the idea of marriage—came back to me with stars in her eyes. It was the first wedding she had been so closely involved in, and she had fallen in love with the idea of it. More than the marriage itself, what she had loved was how family, friends and communities came together on the occasion of a wedding, and suddenly, my family-loving girl wanted to get married too.

'That's not fair,' I said. 'You know very well how I feel about marriage.'

'I was only talking in general,' she said pertly. 'I didn't say I wanted to get married to *you*.'

That shook me up a little. To add to my uneasiness, now that her sister's wedding was done, her parents had turned the spotlight back on us again. Oh well, I said a few months later, when she ooh-ed and aah-ed about marriage again, I certainly don't want you to go off and get married to someone else, so, all right, let's do this.

Getting her dad's blessing took a while—he is an extreme sort of introvert and would not look at me when I went to ask for his daughter's hand, merely grunting in response to anything I said. After making me squirm for a long while, he finally spoke. 'If she is happy,' he mumbled, 'I am happy.' Phewwwwww.

Ankita and I were married in April 2018 in Alibaug. It was a simple, intimate event, with family and a small group of close friends in attendance. The ceremonies were a mix of traditional Maharashtrian and traditional Assamese, as we had wanted. So were our wedding outfits, and who better to design them than my old friend Madhu Jain? For Ankita, Madhu created an organic, handwoven nauvari sari in the Assamese bride's colours of white and gold; for me, the pan-Indian bridegroom's traditional outfit of dhoti and kurta in the same colours. To commemorate the occasion, the two of us, along with our guests, planted 100 trees in the area.

Then, because my wife also wanted a white wedding—these millennials!—we decided to make it something really,

really special. If we had to get married in a church, why not in the eleventh-century Cathedral of Santiago de Compostela in Spain? But of course, it couldn't be that straightforward when I was involved—we would have to earn our white wedding. And we would do that by walking one of the ninth-century pilgrimage routes—part of the network of routes called the Camino de Santiago—to the cathedral. We picked the route that began in Lisbon in Portugal; from the starting point, we would need to walk 600 kilometres in twenty days to get to the cathedral, which worked out to 30 kilometres of walking per day, and how hard could that be? Especially considering that this was a well-worn pilgrimage route equipped with all kinds of infrastructure along the way to make things convenient. We even convinced Aai and my sisters to get on board, although my sisters decided, wisely, that they would only join us in Spain, for the last leg of the trek.

The three of us set off enthusiastically on Day 1 from Lisbon, but Ankita and I realized pretty quickly that there was a great difference between running 30 kilometres and walking 30 kilometres. Walking took too long and used completely different muscles; it was boring and, worse, completely exhausting. We gave up on the idea of walking the whole way on Day 2 or 3—after all, this was also supposed to be a fun family vacation—and took taxis when we could. By Day 20, when we got to the town of Santiago de Compostela, the bride and groom had walked only 410 kilometres in all.

Not so the mother-in-law. At the age of seventy-nine, Aai was always ahead of us, and when we wound up the walking for the day, she was never so tired that she did not, after a quick shower, go out to get an eyeful of the town we were in. But then her body is beautifully conditioned, and has been for years—she walks everywhere when she is home in Bombay, and does a monthly trek in the hills as well. Now you know who to blame for my 'age is just a number' theory.

Netra, Medha and Anupama joined us in Spain as promised, walking the last 118 kilometres with us. With Aai, they also scouted for and found us a beautiful clearing in the middle of a forest, with a waterfall as backdrop, to serve as the natural cathedral in which we may exchange our vows again. My brother-in-law, Ashok, who had graciously agreed to get ordained as a minister of the Universal Life Church (the ULC is a non-denominational religious organization that offers to legally ordain anyone, free of charge, as a priest, so that they may perform the weddings of their friends and family—I found it online), officiated at the ceremony.

As I have said before, I am not the sentimental type, but I have to say that standing there that morning, surrounded by my best girls, in a place hallowed by tradition and blessed by Mother Nature, felt quite, quite perfect.

EPILOGUE

FRESH FIELDS

'And what difference does it make, anyway, what you like and what you don't like? You are here for but an instant, and you mustn't take yourself too seriously.'

—Edgar Rice Burroughs

What's next for you, Milind? I'm often asked. *What's the next big challenge?* I can only answer such questions in the very short term—the next three months, six months, a year. Beyond that, who knows? As I have said before, I am an explorer—I follow the scent.

Here's what I already know I'm chasing, though. Now that Pinkathon is up, up and away and doesn't need my constant involvement, I'm shifting my focus to other kinds of running events. In 2015, I became part of the organizing team of the Coorg Barefoot Marathon, the world's very first run of its kind. This year will be its fifth edition, and it is only going from strength to strength as more and more people discover the joy of connecting with nature while running barefoot.

The year before, we started another annual event, which is held on 30 and 31 December each year, called 'The Last Long Run'—the idea being to do a run of about 150 kilometres over the last two days of the year to end it on a grand note, to make even the last two days count, and then bring in the new year with a fun party at the destination. So far, we've done runs from Bombay to Pune, Bangalore to Mysore, Una to Dharamsala, Goa to Gokarna. In 2018, we ran from Colombo to Unawatuna in Sri Lanka, and in 2019, from Tokyo to Mt Fuji in Japan. For this year's Last Long Run, Cambodia is in our sights. That one's going to be great fun for sure, as it always is.

For some time now, I have been toying with the idea of a Festival of Ancient Wisdom. I see it essentially as a travelling festival, one that travels to geographies and communities worldwide where traditional knowledge has been nurtured and kept alive for hundreds of years. A kind of tribal festival, if you will, which will attempt to bring together, make public and celebrate all kinds of traditional knowledge—more organic, closer to the land, more natural—that have become marginalized because of the kind of monopoly certain kinds of 'approved' or 'modern' knowledge have on our minds.

What else? Oh yes, an initiative called Swavalamban (meaning 'self-reliance') by United Sisters Foundation (USF), the non-profit that organizes Pinkathon. While Pinkathon has not been conceived as a fundraiser, all participants are encouraged to raise money through running the Pinkathon, which is donated directly to the Women's Cancer Initiative in Bombay. Part of that money is now being used by USF to pilot Swavalamban, an initiative to get women of all backgrounds talking about the taboo topic of menstrual health and hygiene, and to raise awareness of these issues among women and girls of disadvantaged and underserved communities.

Apart from these 'organizational' goals, I am chasing some personal ones as well in the short term. I want to send Aai to the World Masters Athletics Championships next year. The World Masters Athletics is considered the Olympics for athletes over thirty-five. Each 'veteran' athlete competes in his or her own age category, and there is no maximum age. I'd love to see Aai compete in a couple of events in the seventy-five-plus age category—I'm sure she will enjoy the experience.

For myself, I want to attempt the Double Ironman Triathlon—two Ironman triathlons over two consecutive days—sometime soon. And of course, one day in the not-too-distant future, I hope to summit Everest.

Why do you take on these extreme challenges? I'm often asked. *Why do you always choose the most difficult way to do things? Why can you not stop wanting to do something more challenging than what you have already done?*

Now those are questions that I can answer. And the simplest, most succinct answer is this—because it's such a massive, glorious head-rush.

You see, there are many routes to wisdom. You will get there whether you take the well-marked, well-ordered, safe and steady route, or the overgrown one that you have to hack through with a machete, while bracing yourself to deal with whatever leaps out at you from the underbrush. My personal head-rush comes from not knowing how much further the path runs or what might be around the next corner, and from knowing for certain that whether you survive it or not, just walking the second route will give you the most dazzling insights and perspectives in the shortest amount of time. You learn the most, you see the most, when you push yourself to the limit.

The ultimate conquest in the world, as our own ancient scriptures agree, is the conquest of the mind. But the mind is a fickle, obstinate, cunning, deluded thing—it is inordinately difficult to conquer the mind via the mind. Thousands of years ago, deep inside our forests and in the high, snowy reaches of our mountains, our ancient sages discovered the explosive truth that the mind was best conquered via the body—they sat or stood, unmoving, for weeks, months, years—systematically defeating hunger, thirst, heat, cold, sleep, proving that the body's 'needs' were nothing more than artificial barriers, constructed entirely by the mind, to fulfilling one's true potential. As those imagined fetters fell away, the lines between mind and body blurred, and the two began to work in perfect synchronicity, each learning from the other instead of holding it back, each complementing the other instead of standing in its way.

When I run, when I undertake extreme physical challenges, I seek that same glorious coming together of physical, mental, emotional and spiritual faculties, that same ecstatic sense of liberation that results when your mind and body work in unison, that the ancient sages experienced. I am nowhere near achieving it, but when I run, I get almost instantly into that meditative headspace, which is the starting point of that great quest, a space where my many minds converge and become focused and still. I use running as a tool to yoke mind and body together—it is a high, and a very addictive one at that.

There's nothing self-indulgent or escapist about this kind of addiction, but could there perhaps be something detrimental about it? What is the point of being amazingly fit, if you end up destroying your body on the way there? What level of fitness is healthy for you? Those are good questions, and valid ones. The debate around them rages, but the jury is still out. Whatever the answer may be, one thing is clear to me: The more you challenge yourself physically, the more you grow strong mentally. Abrade your body by degrees, and by degrees, your mind becomes invincible.

Here's something else I have discovered: When you create efficiency in one area of your life—say physical fitness—using a combination of discipline, doggedness and self-belief, you create efficiency in every other area of your life as well. Keep your body in top condition as a matter of course, and you free your mind up to go after what it really wants. Push your body a little further each day, and watch your self-belief grow stronger and stronger, until it becomes unshakeable. Those are the real reasons I run.

The thing is, you do not need to be especially gifted or talented to achieve this—you just need to be pig-headed, and that is something we are all capable of, especially when it is to do with the things we really care about. And what can be more important than good health, both physical and mental? What is happiness but the knowledge that your body is strong enough and your mind calm enough to take on any challenge that life may throw at you? What is wisdom but the realization that while it is futile to work towards controlling the world, it makes a whole lot of sense to work towards controlling your mind, which is what really constructs your world?

When I was dreaming up Pinkathon, I came up with a tagline that I thought would be perfect for it. We don't use it any more, but to me, it still epitomizes a philosophy that I have lived by my entire life, and one I believe is the cornerstone of a happy life. And this seems as good a time and place as any to share it. It is just four words long—*The Cause*, it states simply, *Is You*.

Who knows what the future holds? All we have is the present, and all we can do is make it as pleasant for ourselves and everyone around us as possible. All we can do is love ourselves so much that we leave the past behind, however terrible or wonderful it may have been. All we can do is stay curious and treat each new day as a great new adventure, packed with the promise of new experiences that may not always be pleasant but are certainly not to be feared.

All we can do is keep moving.

Speaking Minds is an international speakers' bureau, content curator and B2B expert. It has one of the largest varieties of speakers from around the world, and curates cutting-edge B2B events. It also specializes in creating and managing employee and client interventions for corporate companies.

Milind Soman is an exclusive speaker with Speaking Minds. For inquiries, you can write to info@speakingminds.com.